TORRES DEL PAINE

TREKKING IN CHILE'S PREMIER NATIONAL PARK
AND
ARGENTINA'S LOS GLACIARES NATIONAL PARK

About the Author

Rudolf Abraham (www.rudolfabraham.co.uk) is an award-winning writer and photographer whose love of travel and remote places has taken him from the Balkans to eastern Turkey, Central Asia and Patagonia. He is the author of ten books – five of them for Cicerone – and has contributed to many more, and his work is published widely in magazines.

Other Cicerone guides by the author

The Peaks of the Balkans Trail
The Mountains of Montenegro:
    A Walker's and Trekker's Guide
Walking in Croatia
The Islands of Croatia: 30 Walking
    Routes on 14 Adriatic Islands

St Oswald's Way and St Cuthbert's
    Way: Long-distance trails in
    Northumberland and the Borders

TORRES DEL PAINE

TREKKING IN CHILE'S PREMIER NATIONAL PARK

AND

ARGENTINA'S LOS GLACIARES NATIONAL PARK

by Rudolf Abraham

JUNIPER HOUSE, MURLEY MOSS,
OXENHOLME ROAD, KENDAL, CUMBRIA LA9 7RL
www.cicerone.co.uk

Author photo by Ivana Abraham
All other photos by Rudolf Abraham
Printed in China on behalf of Latitude Press Ltd.
A catalogue record for this book is available from the British Library.

For my daughter, Tamara

Acknowledgements

I would like to thank Martina Diez-Routh of Travel Trade UK for her enthusiastic support of this project and for putting me in touch with clients in Chile; Adrien Champagnat, Maria José Eguigoren and Matías del Sol at Remota; André de Mendonça of South American Experience; Anna Francis and Mango PR; Hotel Fundador in Santiago; Alejandro of Hostal la Estancia in Punta Arenas; the Latin American Travel Association (LATA); John Biggar; Lisa Phillips at New Holland Publishers; Vicky Atkins at A & C Black; and Jonathan Williams and all the team at Cicerone. Finally I must thank my wife, Ivana, who checked the language section – and who was with me every step of the way.

Updates to this Guide

While every effort is made by our authors to ensure the accuracy of guidebooks as they go to print, changes can occur during the lifetime of an edition. Any updates that we know of for this guide will be on the Cicerone website (www.cicerone.co.uk/840/updates), so please check before planning your trip. We also advise that you check information about such things as transport, accommodation and shops locally. Even rights of way can be altered over time. We are always grateful for information about any discrepancies between a guidebook and the facts on the ground, sent by email to updates@cicerone.co.uk or by post to Cicerone, Juniper House, Murley Moss, Oxenholme Road, Kendal, LA9 7RL.

Register your book: To sign up to receive free updates, special offers and GPX files where available, register your book at www.cicerone.co.uk.

Front cover: Paine massif from near Lago Toro, Torres del Paine national park, Patagonia, Chile

CONTENTS

The catamaran at Refugio Paine Grande on Lago Pehoé (Walks 1 and 2)

Map Key

═══════	roads
━━━━━━	walking route
━ ━ ━ ━	alternative route
─ ─ ─ ─	national park boundary
▬ ▬ ▬	international border
→ ❷→	direction of route
)(	col or mountain pass
▲	summit
I I	bridge
⛺	camping area
⛺	former campsite (now closed)
⇧	refuge
⬆	hotel
■	other building
〰	lake or reservoir
〰	river or stream
⬜	glacier

Contour colour key

1250–1500m		2750–3000m	
1000–1250m		2500–2750m	
750–1000m		2250–2500m	
500–750m		2000–2250m	
250–500m		1750–2000m	
0–250m		1500–1750m	
sea level			

Torres del Paine national park

N
0   5 km

PERU

BOLIVIA

Antofagasta

CHILE

ARGENTINA

N
0   500 km

Valparaíso
Santiago

Temuco

Puerto Montt

Pacific
Ocean

Los Glaciares
national park
El Calafate

Torres del Paine
national park
Puerto Natales

Punta Arenas

Glaciar Grey

Camp
L
Pe

Paso
John
Gardner

Campamento
Paso

Cerro
Blanco Su

Campamento
Los Guardas

Cerr
Catea

Refugio
Grey

Lago Pingo

Lago Grey

Glaciar Zapata

Campamento Zapata

Campo de Hielo Sur

Hos

Campamento
Pingo

Glaciar
Tyndall

❶ the 'O' circuit

❷ the 'W' circuit

10

Walks described
Other routes

Lago Dickson
Lago Paine
Refugio Dickson
Campamento Serón
Laguna Azul
Río Zamora
Laguna Azul
Río Paine
Campamento Torres
Valle Ascencio
Torre Norte
Torre Central
Refugio El Chileno
Cerro Fortaleza
Torre Sur
Campamento Británico
Refugio Las Torres
Hotel Las Torres
Laguna Amarga
Monte Almirante Nieto
Valle Francés
Refugio Los Cuernos
Guardería Laguna Amarga
Cerro Paine Grande
Campamento Italiano
Lago Nordenskjöld
Portería Sarmiento
Refugio Paine Grande
Pudeto
Lago Sarmiento
Lago Pehoé
Hostería Pehoé
Camping Pehoé
Laguna Verde
Hostería Mirador del Paine
Hotel Explora
Campamento Las Carretas
Posada Río Serrano
CONAF Administracíon
Río Serrano
Lago Toro

11

Fortaleza and Cerro Espada (Walks 1 and 2)

Location of routes

8 **El Chaltén**

Cerro Fitzroy

national park boundary

Lago Viedma

Disputed Border Area

N

0   50 km

ARGENTINA

CHILE

Los Glaciares national park

CAMPO DE HIELO SUR

Lago Argentino

Perito Moreno glacier

El Calafate

Sierra Baguales

Torres del Paine national park

Bernardo O'Higgins national park

1 **2**

7   **3** **6**

Cerro Castillo →

Lago Toro

Cueva del Milodón

Balmaceda glacier

Seno Última Esperanza

Puerto Natales

Balmaceda glacier in Last Hope Sound,
Bernardo O'Higgins national park (Excursion 2)

INTRODUCTION

'These vast piles of snow, which never melt, and seem destined to last as long as the world holds together, present a noble and even sublime spectacle... they may be likened to great frozen Niagaras; and perhaps these cataracts of blue ice are to the full as beautiful as the moving ones of water.'

Charles Darwin, Voyage of the Beagle *(London, 1839)*

Chile's Torres del Paine national park lies towards the southern tip of South America, surrounded on the west by labyrinthine, lonely fjords and on the east by seemingly endless, dry steppe, and sitting on the edge of the Southern Patagonian Ice Field, the largest sheet of ice in the southern hemisphere outside Antarctica.

There is a feeling of immensity in the landscapes of this, Chile's premier national park – vast sheets of fractured blue ice, turquoise- and emerald lakes, primeval-looking forest, vertical granite spires and seemingly limitless cloud-streaked skies. It is one of those rare destinations with which you think you are familiar even before arriving – after all, one or more of its iconic views decorate almost any publication or webpage associated with Patagonia – yet it has somehow managed to lose none of its magic. It is, quite simply, a staggeringly beautiful place.

The Cuernos from near the CONAF office on Lago Toro (Walks 1 and 4)

Trekking in Torres del Paine – a national park since 1959 and a UNESCO Biosphere Reserve since 1978 – is a hugely rewarding experience. The Torres del Paine Circuit (a circuit of the park, and the main route described in this guide) is without any doubt one of the world's truly great treks, an opportunity to travel through awe-inspiring mountain scenery in an area with a fascinating history and rich in wildlife. Trails are for the most part clear and well marked within the national park, there is a comprehensive network of huts and campsites, and transport both to and within the park is all refreshingly simple.

It takes about 10 to 11 days to complete the 140km Torres del Paine Circuit as described here – but bad weather can delay your crossing of the highest point on the route, the 1180m Paso John Gardner. The shorter version of the route, the 'W', requires five days. None of the walking is particularly difficult, and elevation gain is minimal for most of the stages on the route – the exceptions being the hike over the pass, and up the Valle Ascencio and Valle Francés (but be warned, rain and wind can turn either of these treks into a considerably more demanding undertaking). The northern part of the Circuit is also fairly remote, with no convenient exit point should you want or need to cut your walk short. This guide also includes some of the shorter walks in the national park, as well as excursions from the nearby town of Puerto Natales, and a trek in the equally beautiful Fitzroy area of Los Glaciares national park over the border in Argentina.

Torres del Paine takes its name from the magnificent granite spires which launch themselves skyward near the head of the Valle Ascencio (*torres* meaning 'towers') – one of the most iconic sights in Patagonia, or anywhere in South America for that matter – and the name of a local *estancia* (ranch), upon which part of the national park still lies.

The national park does attract an increasingly large number of visitors each year, most of whom arrive in the peak (summer) season of January/February, when the 'W' route can get quite crowded, yet despite this it is still possible to find solitude, particularly in the more northerly areas of the park. On my first visit to Torres del Paine I sat among boulders by a stream in the Valle Francés, mesmerized, as shafts of early morning sunlight struck the enormous east face of Paine Grande, all dark rock slung with glaciers, and glistening crags festooned with clouds. It mattered nothing that there was a campsite with a few dozen tents hidden in the forest behind me; in those few moments I was completely and utterly alone. On another visit I clung to an exposed section of trail in screaming winds, only to turn and see a Condor rising effortlessly out of the valley, utterly still except for the feathers on its wing tips, and so close I almost felt I could reach out and touch it.

Torres del Paine

Place names almost always provide a fascinating window into a region's past. The Paine massif probably takes its name from the Tehuelche world for 'blue', *paine*. The Tehuelche, the indigenous inhabitants of this part of Patagonia, have also left their legacy in other place names (*pehoé* means 'hidden', as in Lago Pehoé; *baguales* means 'wild horses', as in Sierra Baguales – perhaps a clue as to what was so attractive to them that side of the Verlika pass), as well as in the names of various plants and animals. And the correct pronunciation should really be 'pine-ay', not 'pain'.

Patagonia

Patagonia is a region covering the southernmost part of South America, made up of the southern parts of Argentina and Chile. The name 'Patagonia' derives from the description of the native Mapuche population by Antonia Pigafetta, in his record of the voyage of Magellan. Pigafetta described the Mapuche as *'Patagones'*, which has long been considered to have meant 'big feet' or 'big footed' in Spanish – although while *pata* does indeed mean foot, there is no real explanation for the *-gon* suffix. His description gave rise to enduring legends of a race of giants inhabiting the wilds of southern South America. His description tells us as much about the teller as the subject – the average height for an adult male Mapuche was 5' 11", while that of the average Spaniard at that time was 5' 1".

Another more recent explanation for the origins of the word Patagonia is that it comes from a 16th-century Spanish romance, *Primaleón of Greece*, in which the hero encounters a race of 'savages', who ate raw flesh and clothed themselves in animal skins (as did the native population encountered by Pigafetta), including a creature called Patagon, described as strange and misshapen, with 'the face of a dog' and 'teeth sharpe and big' – in other words, all those things the 'civilized' explorer might have expected to encounter in a race of 'savages' at the uttermost ends of the Earth.

GEOGRAPHY AND GEOLOGY

Chile's 4300km-long, stringbean shape encompasses an enormous variety of scenery (not to mention climates), from the parched salt pans and blistering heat of the Atacama desert in the north to the splintered fjords, fractured glaciers and frigid wilds of its far south. Its highly indented coastline runs to over 6400km in length, yet the country is on average only some 175km wide. Far off its coast in the waters of the Pacific, its territory includes the Juan Fernández Archipelago and the ever mysterious Rapa Nui or Easter Island – the latter separated from the Chilean mainland by over 3800km of uninterrupted ocean.

The country is divided into 15 administrative regions, their names preceded by Roman numerals and (with the exception of two regions newly created in 2007) arranged numerically from north to south. Torres del Paine national park lies in the 12th (southernmost) of these regions, XII Región de Magallanes y de la Antártica Chilena, the regional capital of which is Punta Arenas.

Running along (and effectively defining) Chile's eastern border is the Andes mountain range, which stretches some 7000km down the western side of the South American continent and constitutes both the world's longest mountain range and the highest mountain range outside Asia. The highest peak in the Andes (and in the southern hemisphere), Aconcagua (6962m), is located about 100km northeast of the Chilean capital, Santiago, over the border in Argentina; the second highest peak in the Andes, and the highest in Chile, is Nevado Ojos del Salado (6891m), which lies some 600km north of Aconcagua.

Further south, the Andes are generally lower in elevation, with the highest peak in Chilean Patagonia (Monte San Valentin) reaching 4058m; while the highest peak in Torres del Paine national park (Cerro Paine Grande) clocks in at a mere 3050m, or somewhat less according to some measurements. Formed by the movement of the Nazca and Antarctic plates beneath the South American plate, the Andes also contain many volcanoes (Nevado Ojos del Salado for example,

Cerro Paine Grande (Walks 1 and 2)

and the 6570m Tupungato which towers above Santiago) – several of them active (Chile's Llaima volcano erupted in both 2008 and 2009; Chaitén in 2008–9).

Chile's position on the edge of the Pacific plate means that it also experiences its share of earthquakes, including the Great Chilean Earthquake of 1960 which devastated the city of Valdivia and measured a staggering 9.5 on the Moment Magnitude Scale (MMS, a development of the Richter Scale which measures large earthquakes more accurately) – the world's strongest ever recorded. In February 2010 another huge earthquake struck the area south of Santiago, measuring 8.8 on the MMS and causing widespread destruction.

The Andes are rich in mineral resources, and mining is extensive – with Chile ranking as the world's largest copper producer, supplying a third of the world's copper consumption. Argentina is also a major copper producer, while the Bolivian Andes are particularly rich in tin; and historically, it was the mineral wealth of the Andes which supplied the Inca civilization – and later the Conquistadors – with silver and gold.

Torres del Paine national park lies a little under 2000km south of Santiago on the edge of the vast Campo de Hielo Sur or Southern Ice Field, fingers of which (the Grey, Tyndall and Dickson glaciers) penetrate deep into the national park. These feed the lakes and rivers which, in their turn, drain southward into the Seno Ultima Esperanza or Last Hope Sound. The lakes and rivers carry large volumes of suspended particles of rock produced by the action of glaciers ('glacial milk'), and it is this which gives many of the lakes (such as Lago Pehoé and Lago Nordenskjöld) their vivid turquoise hue.

On the trail by Lago Pehoé (Walk 1)

The national park covers an area of some 240,000 hectares, and is roughly delineated by the Chilean-Argentine border and Argentina's Los Glaciares national park to the north, the Río Zamora and the eastern shore of Lago Sarmiento in the east, the Southern Ice Field to the west, and the Río Serrano and the enormous Bernardo O'Higgins national park to the south. The Cordillera del Paine or Paine massif lies more or less at its centre, slightly separate from and to the east of the main Andes chain – a landscape of vertical granite spires and shattered rocky peaks, which emerge above unspoilt forest, fast-flowing mountain streams, spectacularly coloured lakes and massive glaciers.

Much of the Paine massif constitutes the exposed remnants of a granite laccolith – igneous rock, which was injected into the earth's crust some 12 million years ago during the Miocene epoch, forcing the surrounding sedimentary rock upwards. An earlier intrusion (a mafic intrusion of monzonite, and later olivine-gabbro) underpins the granite laccolith. Since then the surrounding sedimentary rock has been gradually eroded, leaving the more resistant granite Torres ('towers') – along with other peaks such as Fortaleza and Cerro Espada – gloriously exposed. This exposed granite also forms the central portion or band of the Cuernos ('horns'), while their dark, spiky upper bands constitute the shattered remnants of the surrounding sedimentary strata. The underlying intrusion is only partially exposed.

The southern portion of the Paine massif is bisected at its centre and towards its eastern side by the two river valleys, the Valle Francés and the Valle Ascencio. Both the Río Francés and the Río Ascencio drain south into Lago Nordenskjöld, which then drains into Lago Pehoé and Lago Toro; on the western side of the massif the huge Glaciar Grey feeds Lago Grey and the Río Grey.

THE SOUTHERN PATAGONIAN ICE FIELD

The Southern Patagonian Ice Field or Campo de Hielo Sur is the largest expanse of ice in the southern hemisphere outside Antarctica, stretching about 350km north to south and covering an area of about 16,800km^2 – some 14,000km^2 of which lies within Chile (predominantly within Bernardo O'Higgins national park), the rest being in Argentina. The average elevation of the Southern Ice Field is about 1400–1600m, though several of the glaciers descend to sea level in the west, and it reaches well over 3000m in places. Largest among its huge glaciers is the Pío XI or Bruggen glacier (the longest in the southern hemisphere outside Antarctica), some 64km long and covering an area of 1265km^2; others include the O'Higgins (820km^2),

Jorge Montt (510km²), Tyndall (331km²) and Grey (270km²) glaciers in Chile, and the Viedma (978km²), Uspala (902km²) and Perito Moreno (258km²) glaciers in Argentina.

In all 48 major outlet glaciers have been identified, together with a further 100 smaller cirque and valley glaciers. Most of the major glaciers either terminate in the sea (on the Chilean side), including the Jorge Montt, Pío XI and the Serrano, or in freshwater lakes such as those in Torres del Paine and Los Glaciares national parks. Only three of these glaciers are not retreating, the Pío XI, San Rafael and the Perito Moreno. Otherwise, the retreat of glaciers in the area has been exceptionally rapid, the Grey some 2.3km and the Tyndall some 1.6km over the past 22 years, and the O'Higgins retreating 14.6km and losing an area of over 50km² in the period 1896 to 1995 – one of the largest glacial retreats of the 20th century. Almost all of the glaciers are calving (shedding huge chunks of ice from their snout), often in spectacular fashion, into adjacent lakes or fjords.

The Southern Patagonian Ice Field forms only one part of what was once the Patagonian Ice Sheet; the North Patagonian Ice Field (now contained within the area of Chile's Laguna San Rafael national park) is the other, smaller, remaining portion. About 17,500–18,000 years ago, during the last glacial period (the Llanquihue glaciation, as it is called in Chile), the Patagonian Ice Sheet covered an area of some 480,000km², stretching roughly as far north as Puerto Montt, and also extended across the Andes some distance into Argentina.

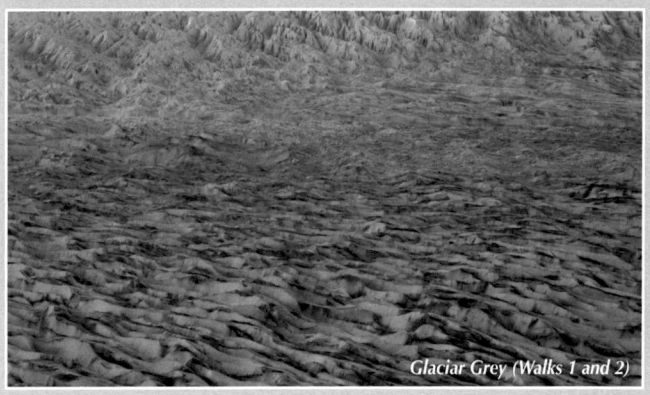

Glaciar Grey (Walks 1 and 2)

CLIMATE

The 16th-century English navigator and adventurer Thomas Cavendish had little positive to say for the Patagonian climate, describing it (or more specifically, the conditions he encountered in the Straits of Magellan) as 'vile and filthy foul weather'. This is a little harsh, however, for while it is true there can be plenty of wind and rain in this part of the world, the climate isn't always that grim. In Torres del Paine national park, days are long during the summer, and the weather can be wonderful, with some of the most magnificent cloud formations. You just need to come prepared for, well, foul weather.

Daytime temperatures in January/February (that is, summer in the southern hemisphere) in Torres del Paine average around 11°C, although it can vary enormously from around 24°C to just above freezing, and at night will feel much cooler. Precipitation levels also vary, generally increasing further west, and in proximity to the South Patagonian Ice Field.

Weather conditions in Torres del Paine are notoriously difficult to predict, the huge glaciers in the area giving rise to various microclimates, which make accurate long-term weather forecasts almost impossible.

One thing trekkers have to get used to in Torres del Paine is the wind, which fairly blasts off the South Patagonian Ice Field straight into the Paine massif, and when it gets really strong (gusts of well over 100km/h are not uncommon) it can make walking almost impossible. Huts carry

*Lone Ñirre (*Nothofagus antarctica*) and low cloud, near Mirador Cuernos (Walk 3)*

Windswept trees near Glaciar Los Perros (Walk 1)

(tentative) forecasts for at least two or three days ahead, so it's worth checking these and timing certain sections of your route – such as the crossing of Paso John Gardner – accordingly. Of course it's not always windy, and there are plenty of days when it's perfectly calm – although if you get round the entire Circuit without getting at least one day of high winds, not to mention a good dousing of rain, you can count yourself fairly lucky.

The wind is at its worst during the peak visitor months of January and February – conditions tend to be rather more settled (albeit obviously much colder) during the winter. But, to quote the excellent local magazine *Black Sheep* (which has now sadly folded): 'Wind is as much a character [of] the landscape as the mountains, trees and pampas themselves...Prepare yourself as best you can, arm yourself with a good attitude, and enjoy.' Sound advice.

Further north in Chile the climate is very different, with average daytime temperatures in Santiago during the summer reaching around 29°C. The Argentinian side of the border tends to be drier, and it is possible to travel from clear skies and brilliant sunshine in Los Glaciares national park to low cloud and rain in Torres del Paine national park.

When to visit

The trekking season in Torres del Paine lasts roughly from early summer to early autumn (late November to late April). January and February are peak season, coinciding with

23

school holidays in Chile, and during these months campsites and trails can become quite crowded, especially on the more popular 'W' route. Mosquitoes are at their worst at this time. March is on balance the best month to visit, although December and even April are also good. During the winter bitter temperatures and heavy snowfall put most people off, but this can also be a beautiful time to visit (some agencies offer winter ski touring) – and free from the wind and mosquitoes.

WILDLIFE AND PLANTS

Mammals

Almost synonymous with images of Torres del Paine national park is the Guanaco (*Lama guanacoe*), a large cameloid closely related to the Llama. Around the approaches to the national park they have become rather used to busloads of visitors jumping out to take photographs of them. However, in more remote areas such as Sierra Baguales, where humans remain much more of a novelty, they tend to be rather more inquisitive. The calves are born during the spring, and are known locally as *chulengo*. The word 'guanaco' is pronounced with the accent on second syllable.

The other two South American cameloids, the Llama (*Lama glama*) and the Vicuña (*Vicugna vicugna*), are present in other parts of Chile; the Guanaco and the Llama are the slightly larger of the three. There is a fourth cameloid in Chile, the Alpaca (*Lama pacos*), although this is actually a domesticated and selectively bred form of the Vicuña.

Far more elusive is the now endangered Huemul (*Hippocamelus bisulcus*). This small, shy, deer-like animal was once quite common, but was hunted to near extinction by early settlers and is now extremely rare. Male Huemul are slightly larger than the female and stand up to about 90cm at the shoulder. CONAF (Corporación Nacional Forestal), which oversees Chile's national parks, asks that any Huemul sightings are reported to the national park office. The Huemul was incorporated into the Chilean coat of arms in 1834 and still appears there, alongside the Condor. The Southern Pudu (*Pudu puda*), the world's smallest deer, is present in other parts of Chile but not in Torres del Paine.

The largest predatory land mammal in Chile is the Puma (*Puma concolor*) – a beautiful, lithe and (despite the fact that it seems to decorate half the tourist literature of Patagonia) highly elusive big cat. In the highly unlikely event that you see a Puma, count yourself lucky! On a more practical note, if you do happen to meet one and it doesn't run first, do not run, but maintain eye contact and back away slowly, raising your arms to make yourself look as large as possible. Never approach cubs. Also present in the park is the much smaller Geoffroy's Cat or *Gato montés* (*Leopardus (Oncifelis) geoffroyi*),

Guanaco (Lama guanacoe), Sierra Baguales (Excursion 3)

which may be threatened with extinction in the near future.

Two species of fox are present in the park, the South American Grey Fox or *Chilla* (*Lycalopex griseus*; also known as the Patagonian Grey Fox, Zorro Gris or Zorro Patagónico) and the Fuegian Fox or *Culpeo* (*Lycalopex culpaeus*; also known as Zorro Rojo). The *Culpeo* is the larger of the two species, which is also easily distinguished (as the name implies) by the colour of its coat. Both species are protected in Chile, although illegal hunting still occurs. The genus *Dusicyon* is often used for South American foxes instead of *Lycalopex*.

Other mammals include the Big Hairy Armadillo (*Chaetophractus villosus*), Humbolt's Hog-nosed Skunk (*Conepatus humboldtii*), and various species of rodent, including the Long-tailed Colilargo (*Oligoryzomys longicaudatus*), the Patagonian Chinchilla Rat (*Euneomys chinchilloides*) and several species of field and grass mice, such as the Yellow-nosed Akodont (*Abrothrix xanthorhinus*) and the Olive-coloured Akodont (*Abrothrix olivaceus*).

In neighbouring Bernardo O'Higgins national park you have a chance of spotting the Southern Sea Lion (*Otaria flavescens*), South American Fur Seal (*Arctocephalus australis*) and Marine Otter (*Lontra felina*).

Birds

Along with the Guanaco, another familiar wildlife sight in and around Torres del Paine is the Ñandú or Lesser Rhea (*Pterocnemia pennata*), a very large flightless bird with long legs and neck and three toes.

Perhaps the most iconic bird in South America, the Andean Condor or *Cóndor* (*Vultur gryphus*), is also one you have a fairly good chance of seeing in and around the park, soaring on thermal air currents. With a wing-span of up to 310cm, the Condor is the largest flighted landbird. Adults have black plumage with white areas on the back of the wings and around the base of the neck, and bare pinkish skin on the head and neck; adult males have a dark red comb. Appearing clumsy on the ground, the Condor is a magnificent bird once in flight, gliding effortlessly in search of carrion. It usually nests on ledges on cliffs.

The Southern Crested Caracara or *Carancho* (*Polyborus plancus*) is a commonly seen raptor, often spotted by the roadside when driving in southern Chile. It is a striking bird, dusky in colour with cream throat and barred breast, and reddish skin on its face. Less common are the smaller tawny-coloured Chimango

Caracara (*Milvago chimango*) and the comparatively rare White-Throated Caracara or *Carancho cordillerano del sur* (*Phalcoboenus albogularis*). Other birds of prey include the American Kestrel or *Cernícalo* (*Falco sparverius*), sometimes called the Sparrow Hawk (but unrelated to the Sparrowhawk found in the UK), and the Black-Chested Buzzard Eagle or *Calquín* (*Geranoaetus melanoleucus*) – the largest hawk in Chile, adults being recognisable by their black head and throat.

Owls include the Magellanic Horned Owl or *Tucúquere* (*Babu magellanicus*), the largest in the region, with large ear tufts and predominantly grey, mottled plumage, and the smaller and more common Austral Pygmy-Owl or *Chuncho* (*Glaucidium nanum*).

The Chilean Flamingo or *Flamenco chileno* (*Phoenicopterus chilensis*) is found on or around lakes with a high alkaline or salt content such as Laguna Amarga and Laguna Los Cisnes.

The Black-necked Swan or *Cisne de cuello negro* (*Cygnus melancoryphus*) is frequently seen along the shores of Last Hope Sound near Puerto Natales, or Laguna de los Juncos or Lago Toro within the park. Slightly less

Male Upland Goose or Caiquén (Chleophaga picta)

Carancho or Southern Caracara (Caracara plancus)

common is the Coscoroba or *Cisne coscoroba* (*Coscoroba coscoroba*), a smaller all-white swan with a reddish bill. The Upland Goose or *Caiquén* (*Chloephaga picta*) is another common resident in and around the park; the male is predominantly white with a black barred breast, and the female predominantly cinnamon-brown with black barred flanks. The slightly smaller Ashy-headed Goose (*Chloephaga poliocephala*) is also fairly common.

The Crested Duck (*Lophonetta specularioides*), Andean Ruddy Duck (*Oxyura ferruginea*), Chiloe Wigeon (*Anas sibilatrix*) and Speckled Teal (*Anas flavirostris*) are all fairly common residents in the park. Less common are the Spectacled or Bronze-winged Duck (*Speculanus specularis*) and

Flying steamer-Duck (*Tachyeres patachonicus*), both of which can be seen on Lago Toro, the Cinnamon Teal (*Anas cyanoptera*) and the rather wonderful Torrent Duck or *Pato cortacorrientes* (*Merganetta armata*), which can be spotted perched on rocks in some of the more remote, fast-running mountain streams, such as the upper reaches of Río Ascensio (see photo p87)

The Black-faced Ibis or *Bandurria* (*Theristicus melanopis*), with its long curved bill, ochre neck and grey band across its breast, is often seen in fairly large groups, grazing in open meadows within the park. (The Buff-necked Ibis, *Theresticus caudatus*, is very similar but lacks the grey band.)

The Neotropic Cormorant or *Yeco* (*Phalacrocorax brasilianus*) is found in the larger rivers and lakes in and around the park; it is glossy black, with a small area of white plumage around the bill during the breeding season. Its call is fairly distinctive, a series of rather pig-like grunts. Also resident in larger lakes and rivers is the Great Grebe or *Huala* (*Podiceps major*), large and fairly long-necked, with dark grey to black plumage and a red-brown patch on its neck. Much smaller and somewhat less common is the Silvery Grebe or *Blanquillo* (*Podiceps occipatalis*). The Blue-eyed or Imperial Cormorant (*Phalacrocorax atriceps*) is found in Bernardo O'Higgins national park, and can be seen on the cliffs of Last Hope Sound between Puerto Natales and the Balmaceda glacier.

The Southern Lapwing, also called the *Queltehue* or *Tero*

(*Vanellus chilensis*) is another common resident, as are the Magellanic Oystercatcher or *Pilpilén austral* (*Haematopus leucopodus*) and the South American Snipe (*Gallinago paraguaiae*). Two gulls are found in the national park, the Kelp Gull (*Larus dominicanus*) and the Brown-hooded Gull (*Larus maculipennis*).

Woodpeckers include the Magellanic Woodpecker or *Carpintero negro* (*Campephilus magellanicus*), a large and truly magnificent-looking bird, black-bodied with a white 'v'-shaped marking on its back and, in the case of the male, a brilliant red head; and the smaller Striped Woodpecker or *Carpinterito chico* (*Picoides lignarius*). The Chilean Flicker or *Pitío* (*Colaptes pitius*) is fairly common in the park. The Green-backed Firecrown (*Sephanoides sephanoides*), a member of the hummingbird family, is sometimes seen in the Valle Francés.

Other common species include the Rufous-collared Sparrow or *Chincol* (*Zonotrichia capensis*), the Austral Blackbird or *Tordo* (*Curaeus curaeus*), the Patagonian Sierra-Finch (*Phrygilus patagonicus*) and the Grey-hooded Sierra Finch (*Phrygilus gayi*).

*Magellanic Penguin (*Spheniscus magellanicus*) and burrow*

WHERE TO WATCH WILDLIFE

For birdwatchers, some of the best areas in the Torres del Paine national park are Lago Toro and the smaller lakes and pools between Pudeto and Laguna Amarga (such as Laguna Los Cisnes and Laguna Los Juncos); the area surrounding the latter is also a good area for spotting Guanaco. Laguna Amarga is one of the best areas in the park for seeing Chilean Flamingos. On the Torres del Paine Circuit, Torrent Ducks may be spotted in the upper reaches of the Río Ascencio. Some of the less-visited areas of the national park such as Río Pingo offer a good chance of seeing wildlife and birdlife, including some of the less common species – if you're really lucky, you may spot a Huemúl. The best place to see Magellanic Penguins is on Isla Magdalena, about 2hrs by boat from Punta Arenas in the Straits of Magellan.

The Magellanic Penguin (*Spheniscus magellanicus*) is present in Bernardo O'Higgins national park, and in huge numbers (some 120,000) on Isla Magdalena, in the Straits of Magellan. While in the Straits of Magellan you also have a chance of spotting the Black-browed Albatross (*Thalassarche melanophris*) and the Southern Giant-Petrel (*Macronectes giganteus*).

Reptiles and amphibians

The park is home to several species of amphibian including the Grey Four-eyed Frog (*Pluerodema bufoninum*), Grey Wood Frog (*Batrachyla nibaldoi*), the Spiny-chest Frog (*Alsodes australis*) and the Patagonian Toad (*Chaunus (Bufo) variegatus*). Reptiles include the Magellanic Lizard (*Liolaemus magellanicus*), Fitzinger's Lizard (*Liolaemus fitzingeri*) and the rather wonderfully named Darwin's Grumbler (*Diplolaemus darwinii*).

Invertebrates

At least ten species of butterfly have been recorded in the national park, including Whites and Fritillary; less pleasantly, huge numbers of particularly voracious mosquitoes are present during the summer. The Black Widow spider has been found in some localised areas of the park, including around Laguna Amarga.

Plants

The dense deciduous forests of Torres del Paine national park are characterized by several species of Southern Beech, primarily Lenga (*Nothofagus pumilio*). The *Lenga* is a tall and fairly broad-trunked tree and grows up to 30m, forming a dense canopy on mountain slopes with plenty of rainfall; it may also occur in a dwarf form. The *Lenga* was the preferred wood for making bows among the Indians of Tierra del Fuego. The Magellanic Coigüe or *Coigüe de magallanes*

1 *Berries of Murta or Prickly Heath (Gaultheria mucronata), Torres del Paine national park*

2 *Estrellita or Falkland Lavender (Perezia recurvata), Torres del Paine national park*

3 *Llareta or Balsam Bog (Bolax gummifera)*

4 *Flowers of Murta or Prickly Heath (Gaultheria mucronata), Torres del Paine national park*

5 *Campanilla or Streaked Maiden (Olsynium biflorum), Torres del Paine national park*

(*Nothofagus betuloides*) is also found on humid mountain slopes with heavy precipitation, as well as on more sheltered areas of scrub. It grows up to about 25m in height or may occur as a shrub. The Antarctic Beech or Ñirre (*Nothofagus antarctica*) grows at lower altitudes or in boggy, water-logged or windy areas. The trunk is often twisted and contorted. It reaches up to 15m in height and occurs as a smaller shrub.

A number of semi-parasitic shrubs are found on the branches of *Northofagus* trees, all (rather confusingly) known as *Farolito chino* in Chile. These include the yellowish *Misodendrum punctulatum* and the green *Misodendrum linearifolium*. Both have shaggy, beard-like appendages, longer in the latter species

and forming a distinctive sight on Northofagus trees in the area.

The Calafate or *Palo amarillo* (*Berberis microphylla*) is a large, bush-like shrub found in and around the park, on scrub and steppe as well as in areas of *Northofagus* forest. The deep bluish berries are edible, and are used to make jam as well as a liqueur (which you'll find for sale in plenty of shops in Puerto Natales). There is a saying here, that whoever eats Calafate berries will one day return to Patagonia (well, it worked for me). The flowers are small and yellow. Not to be confused with the Calafate is the Prickly Heath or *Murta* (*Gaultheria mucronata*), which has small bell-like white flowers and red berries, or the Diddle-Dee or *Murtilla de magallanes* (*Empetrum rubrum*), which has tiny

Lago Toro and Mata Barrosa (Mulinum spinosum) from near Puente Weber (Walk 4)

31

Colourful houses in the old town of Valparaíso, a UNESCO World Heritage Site

fleshy leaves and reddish berries that darken as they ripen. Both these species are found in areas of scrub as well as *Northofagus* forest.

The Firebush or *Notro* (*Embothrium coccineum*), a large bush with bright crimson flowers, grows in scrubland areas such as along the trail north of Refugio Paine Grande and alongside Lago Pehoé. Another common scrub-dwelling species is the white-flowered Fachine or *Mata verde* (*Chiliotrichum diffusum*).

Typical of wet and boggy areas, as well as areas of scrub and steppe, is Balsam Bog or *Llareta* (*Bolax gummifer*), which grows in large (up to 0.5m), deep green semi-hemispherical cushions. Although they look incredibly hardy, they can take up to 10 years to regenerate from a single

human footprint – so tread carefully. Sphagum Moss (*Sphagnum magellanicum*) is also found in bogs and waterlogged areas. On drier, rocky scrub you will find Mata Barrosa (*Mulinum spinosum*), which forms dense thorny cushions up to 0.8m in height, with tiny yellowish flowers.

Flowers in scrub, steppe and rocky areas include the small blue Estrellita or Falkland Lavender (*Perezia recurvata*), the Campanilla or Streaked Maiden (*Olsynium biflorum*), Adesmia or *Chinita dorada* (*Adesmia pumila*) and Saxífraga (*Saxifraga magellanica*).

HISTORY AND CULTURE
Early settlers
By around 12,000BC the great migration of peoples over the land bridge

that once existed between what is now Siberia and Alaska, and down through North and South America, had reached what is now Chile – including its far south. Initially nomadic hunter-gatherers, these peoples nevertheless left a legacy of handicrafts and pottery (see exhibits in the Museo Chileno de Arte Precolombino in Santiago), and the tribes in northern Chile are thought to have had cultural links with local Pre-Incan cultures. The tribes of central Chile appear to have become increasingly settled, with the development of agriculture and irrigation, while those further south in Patagonia and Tierra del Fuego, conditioned by the harsher lanscape and climate, maintained a more nomadic existence.

Excavations in Chile's Cueva del Milodón and surrounding caves, just south of Torres del Paine national park, have unearthed arrowheads indicating human settlement in the area from around 10,000BC. Over the border in Argentina, Cueva de las Manos, near Los Glaciares national park, contains paintings dating back some 9500–13,000 years, including hunting scenes with humans and animals and, later, numerous hands, both imprinted directly onto the cave wall and 'sprayed' in negative, probably from a blow pipe.

Inca Empire and Spanish conquest
During the 15th century the Inca Empire expanded its territory dramatically from Peru, exacting tribute from the tribes of northern Chile, but

House near Lago Toro, Torres del Paine national park (Walks 1 and 4)

met with fierce resistance from the Mapuche, one of the most powerful tribes in central Chile, and the border between Inca and Mapuche lands was fixed on the Río Maule, approximately 250km south of Santiago.

Christopher Columbus' 'discovery' of the Americas in 1492 and Ferdinand Magellan's successful navigation of the Straits of Magellan in 1520 were followed by the Spanish conquest of the Aztec and Inca civilizations in Mexico and Peru (in 1521 and 1532 respectively), the latter under the command of Francisco Pizzaro and Diego de Almagro. Almargo continued south in search of further gold and riches, but finding none turned back at the Aconcagua valley.

In 1538 Pedro de Valdivia, one of Pizzaro's generals, with only a handful of men (Chile's apparent lack of gold or other riches made it a far less attractive proposition to most than Peru), set off southwards from Cuzco in Peru, founding the city of Santiago in 1541. The development of the Chilean capital, at that time still subject to the Viceroyalty of Peru, is well illustrated in a series of plaques on the pavement in Santiago's Plaza de Armas.

Over the following years Valdivia attempted to increase Spanish lands further south, where it was once again the Mapuche who put up fierce resistance, and Valdivia himself was killed in battle by the great Mapuche chief Lautano – it is said, by having molten gold poured down his throat. Nevertheless, further subjugation of the local Chilean population continued after Valdivia's death, and the foundations of colonial society were steadily laid. This resulted in the emergence of powerful landowners and estates worked by a disempowered

Estancia Cerro Paine, on the road to Refugio Las Torres (Walk 2)

native workforce, the decimation of the indigenous population by diseases from Europe, and the conquered people's gradual conversion to Christianity by the Catholic Church.

Fight for independence

Over time Chilean demographics changed, with an increasing number of *mestizos* (those born of Spanish fathers and indigenous mothers) and *criollos* (Spaniards born in Chile) in the population, and with these changes came the fledgling desire for increased autonomy from Spain.

The catalyst for Chile's transition to independence was the Napoleonic conquest of Spain and deposition of the Spanish monarchy. In 1810, at a meeting of prominent citizens in Santiago, a junta was elected, with the purpose of maintaining Spanish sovereignty in Chile. Then, in 1811, José Miguel Carrera took power into his own hands, creating a Chilean flag and a provisional constitution; in response, Royalist troops loyal to Spain were dispatched to Chile from Peru. The junta voted to replace the authoritarian Carrera with the brilliant young general Bernardo O'Higgins, but Carrera retook power, and by failing to send reinforcements to O'Higgins ensured his defeat by Royalists at Rancagua. O'Higgins and other 'Patriots' were forced to escape to Argentina, while numerous others were exiled to the Juan Fernández archipelago, and in Santiago the Royalists reversed the junta's reforms.

Across the Andes, O'Higgins joined forces with the Argentine general José San Martín, who was preparing to drive the Royalists out of South America. San Martín's 'Army of the Andes' and O'Higgins' Patriots launched their offensive in February 1817, crossing the mountains from Mendoza by four different passes and routing the Royalists at the Battle of Chacabuco, and then again at the Battle of Maipú. Chilean independence was declared in April 1818, with the task of leadership passing to O'Higgins (the position was offered to San Martín, but he declined). The Royalists in Peru were soon defeated, although Spain did not recognize Chilean independence until 1840.

The 19th century

O'Higgins ruled until 1823, but the taxes introduced to rebuild the country's war-ravaged economy, and his anti-clerical reforms, made his position increasingly untenable, and he finally went into exile in Argentina, where he died in 1842. There followed an unsettled period, until stability was restored under the authoritarian rule of Diego Portales in 1829. Portales consolidated his position by issuing a new constitution, giving the head of state increased power, and maintaining the support of landowners and clergy, astutely judging it neccessary to overturn those reforms which threatened Church privileges, but he was assassinated in 1837 following his declaration of war on Peru.

Immigration to Chile from Europe increased from the mid-19th century, both in the capital and further south, with several thousand Germans settling in the Chilean Lake District, (the area north of Puerto Montt), and a steady stream of Italian, Croatian, English and other settlers arriving in Patagonia – a process nicely encapsulated in the atmospheric cemetery in Punta Arenas, with its broad, cypress-lined avenues and its gravestones of pioneers and immigrants. Like the earlier process of colonization, this later immigration resulted in the almost complete loss of southern Chile's indigenous population – the Tehuelche and, further south around the coast, the Kaweshkar – who were, quite simply, subsumed beneath the tide of settlers and missionaries. Meanwhile silver and, in particular, copper mining increased in the north, and wheat exports soared, feeding a growing economy and increased international trade.

A lucrative nitrate industry, centred around Antofagusta – at that time part of Bolivia (but now in the north of Chile) – was the cause of Chile's involvement in the War of the Pacific in 1879. Following Bolivia's decision to raise export taxes on nitrate (contrary to an agreement to which an earlier border settlement had been subject), Chile invaded Bolivia, with Peru (which controlled the nitrate-rich area around Iquique and Arica) joining on Bolivia's side soon after. Chile's victory over Bolivia in August 1879, and the capitulation of Lima early in 1881, gave the country a vast area of new territory in the north (the border moved some 900km further north, at both Bolivia's and Peru's expense) and complete control over the enormous nitrate deposits of the Atacama desert. It also cut off Bolivia's access to the Pacific.

Territorial disputes between Chile and Argentina, primarily over Patagonia, were mostly resolved when the two countries signed a treaty of 1881 recognizing their mutual border – although one 50km section of this, just north of Torres del Paine, remains unresolved. (Although the two governments agreed on the position of the border in 1991, this was not ratified by the Argentine parliament, and at the time of writing no formal agreement had been concluded.)

In 1890 the authoritarian president José Manuel Balmaceda's decision to act in direct defiance of Congress led to Civil War, with the army backing Balmaceda and the navy backing Congress. Following his defeat, Balmaceda committed suicide.

The 20th century

Chilean society remained deeply divided, with a vast gap between the disempowered workers and the ruling and landed elite, and strikes became increasingly common, typically resulting in brutal oppression. A number of social reforms were introduced by president Arturo Alessandri in a new constitution in 1925, a theme which was to be taken further by a later president, Eduardo Frei, in the 1960s.

Following his election as Chile's first socialist president in 1970, Salvador Allende instigated a series of radical social reforms aimed at closing the gulf between rich and poor, nationalizing companies and redistributing land. Despite initial successes, however, rising inflation and a drastic fall in world copper prices, combined with covert operations by the CIA to destabilize Allende's government, led to a military coup in 1973, in which Allende was killed in the Moneda Palace when it was bombed.

The 1973 coup ushered in 17 years of brutal military dictatorship under Auguste Pinochet, in which thousands were executed or tortured, opposition parties banned, press freedom curtailed and Congress dissolved. Pinochet's re-privatization of industry and other free-market economic policies eventually led to a reduction in unemployment and inflation, but only at the expense of welfare and education and at massive social cost. Pinochet drafted a new constitution in 1980, which guaranteed him power for a further eight years, following which a referendum would be held.

The referendum of 1988 saw Pinochet voted out of power and a return to democracy under Patricio Aylwin, and both he and his successors Eduardo Frei and Ricardo Lagos attempted to tackle the thorny issue of human rights abuses under Pinochet and to reform the long-neglected health and education sectors.

Chile today

Today Chile has a strong economy – one of the healthiest in South America – although the distribution of wealth remains very uneven, as attested by the shanty towns south of Santiago. In 2006 Michelle Bachelet was elected President – the first woman to hold this position in Chile – and in 2009 Chile became the first South American country to gain full membership of the Organisation for Economic Co-operation and Development. Bachelet was succeeded by Sebastián Piñera in 2010, but returned to office in 2014.

UNESCO WORLD HERITAGE SITES IN CHILE

- Chiloé churches
- Rapa Nui national park (Easter Island)
- Valparaíso old city centre
- Humberstone and Santa Laura saltpetre works
- Sewell mining town
- Qhapaq Ñan, Andean Road System

Torres del Paine national park, though submitted to the tentative list in 1994, is yet to be accepted pending a resolution of the Chilean-Argentine border dispute.

EARLY EXPLORATION AND MOUNTAINEERING

The Southern Patagonian Ice Field was first explored in detail by Federico Reichert in 1913–14. Alberto de Agostini followed in 1928 and 1931, and in 1928–29 Gunter Plüschow undertook an aerial exploration, the aircraft later crashing in Lago Argentino. H.W. Tilman and Jorge Quinteros crossed the Ice Field from east to west in 1955–56, starting from Tilman's yacht 'Mischief', moored in the Chilean fjords, and the two ending up swimming in Lago Argentino before returning.

Eric Shipton visited the area in 1960–61, completing an epic crossing from north to south between the Jorge Montt glacier and Lago Argentino (a distance of over 200km). The first full north–south crossing of the Southern Patagonian Ice Field was completed by Pablo Besser, Mauricio Rojas, José Montt and Rodrigo Fica in 1998. Cerro Lautaro, an active 3380m volcano in Bernardo O'Higgins national park (named after the Mapuche military leader who defeated Valdivia), was first climbed in 1964 by Pedro Skvarca and Luciano Pera.

The first European to see and describe Torres del Paine was Lady Florence Dixie who, bored with England, passed this way on horseback in the 1870s, and described the region in her book *Across Patagonia* (1880): 'Beyond the hills rose the three red peaks and the Cordilleras. Their white glaciers, with the white clouds resting on them, were all mirrored to marvellous perfection in the motionless lake, whose crystal waters were of the most extraordinarily brilliant blue I have ever beheld.' Baquedano Santiago Zamora, Tomás Rogers and Carl Skottsberg all visited the area during the late 19th and early 20th centuries. The great Swedish explorer Otto Nordeskjöld visited the area in the 1920s, followed in the 1930s–40s by the Silesian priest and mountaineer Alberto de Agostini – hence the names Lago Nordeskjöld and Torre di Agostini.

A cattle ranch was established in Torres del Paine in 1896, running until the 1970s, and a large area of the national park on the eastern side still lies on private land. Part of the area was declared a national park in 1959 (although not before large tracts had been cleared for livestock), this being enlarged over the following years until reaching its present size of over 240,000 hectares. It was declared a UNESCO World Biosphere Reserve in 1978.

Climbing expeditions to Torres del Paine began in earnest in the late 1950s, following on the heels of several expeditions to the Fitzroy area of Los Glaciares national park in Argentina a few years earlier. These included Lionel Terray and Guido Magnone on Fitzroy in 1952; Walter Bonatti on the western side of Cerro Torre and the Adele Cordón, and on Cerro Mariano Moreno, in 1958–59; and Cesare Maestri's much disputed climb on Cerro Torre in 1959. Torres del Paine's North Tower (Torre Norte) was first climbed by Guido Monzino in 1957–58; the Central Tower (Torre Central) by Chris Bonington and Don Whillans in 1963; and the South Tower (Torre Sur) by Armando Aste, also in 1963. Fortaleza, at the head of the Valle Francés, was climbed by a British team in 1968.

GETTING TO CHILE

The most direct route is to fly to Santiago (17hrs from the UK, 11hrs from New York, 13hrs from Los Angeles, 16hrs from Sydney, 12hrs from Auckland), and from there to Punta Arenas (3hrs 30mins), from where it's a 3hr bus trip to Puerto Natales, the 'gateway' town for the Torres del Paine national park. Chile's

national carrier, LAN (www.lan.com), tends to offer the best fares, and (at least in my experience) in-flight comfort and entertainment aboard LAN is way ahead of the main competitor on this route, Iberia (www.iberia.com).

Fares are not cheap – expect to pay at least £900 for a return flight from the UK or the US to Santiago in season, and a further £300 for the return flight on to Punta Arenas. LAN sometimes offers promotional fares on domestic flights, but these are not usually available very far in advance, so if you are tying in domestic flight times and dates to an international flight, it's safer to just book the whole flight (international and domestic) at once (unless you are flexible with your itinerary). Check the individual airlines' websites, as well as search engines such as Opodo (www.opodo.com) and

Approaching El Chaltén, Los Glaciares national park, Argentina (Walk 8)

agencies in the UK (see 'Agencies and tour operators' below) to find the best deal. Book as early as possible, particularly for travel in January/February (when flights between Santiago and Punta Arenas often become fully booked).

The majority of flights from the UK and elsewhere in Europe to Chile are routed via Madrid (TAM flies via Sao Paulo), and include a fairly lengthy transit time to get from one terminal/gate to another – however, Madrid airport is huge, and the time taken to get between terminals and gates (which usually includes passing through another security check) should not be underestimated.

Alternatively, you could fly to Santiago and continue from there to Puerto Montt (14hrs by bus, 1hr 40mins by plane), and from there take the Navimag ferry (www.comapa.com) down the Chilean coast to Puerto Natales (3 days). The ferry trip provides a spectacular cruise alongside the Chilean fjords, passing glaciers, icebergs and the occasional whale en route. There is one section of the route which passes slightly further out to sea, however, and if the weather's rough, you can expect a heaving swell.

Another option is to fly to Argentina – via Buenos Aries (17hrs from the UK) and El Calafate (a further 3hrs), which gives you the opportunity to visit Los Glaciares national park (in particular the Fitzroy area near El Chaltén, which unlike the Perito Moreno glacier cannot be visited as a day trip from Puerto Natales), before continuing to Puerto Natales by bus (5hrs), passing through Río Turbio before crossing the border at Dorotea. It is also possible to take a more direct route from El Calafate to Torres del Paine, via the border post at Cerro Castillo, thus completely bypassing Puerto Natales – although in this writer's opinion it would be a great shame to do so. Note that public transport on the latter route is much more limited, and involves changing buses at Cerro Castillo. Airlines flying from the UK to Buenos Aires include Aerolinias Argentinas (www.aerolineas.com.ar), Iberia (www.iberia.com) and British Airways (www.ba.com, via San Paolo).

For the majority of people visiting Torres del Paine from the UK and Europe, travelling to Chile by air will be the only practical option. However there are a number of cruise ships operating around the coast of South America, including between Buenos Aires and Santiago.

TRANSPORT WITHIN CHILE

Travelling within Chile is a refreshingly straightforward affair. LAN (www.lan.com) covers the country with a comprehensive network of domestic flights, and there is another private airline, Sky (www.skyairline.cl). Buses are comfortable, frequent and reliable, and fares very reasonable; and ferries connect various ports along the coast.

Punta Arenas to Puerto Natales

Buses pick up from Punta Arenas airport on their way to Puerto Natales (3hrs, several buses daily); or you could take a short ride by shuttle bus or taxi into Punta Arenas itself, and catch the bus there. If you plan to pick up the bus at the airport, rather than in Punta Arenas, you are advised to book tickets in advance in high season. From Puerto Natales it's a further bus ride (2hrs 30mins – 4hrs) into Torres del Paine national park. See Appendix A for further details of arrival (and bus companies) in Punta Arenas and Puerto Natales, and see 'Transport to and around the park' for details of buses from Puerto Natales to Torres del Paine.

For those heading from Santiago to Puerto Montt (to catch the ferry from there to Puerto Natales), as well as buses and domestic flights, there's also a train as far as Temuco (11hrs), from where you can continue by bus.

There are plenty of car hire companies in Chile (offices in Santiago, Punta Arenas, Puerto Natales etc; see Appendix A). In both Chile and Argentina, you drive on the right.

AGENCIES AND TOUR OPERATORS

The following list covers a selection of tour operators and travel agencies specializing in South America or offering itineraries in Torres del Paine and Los Glaciares national parks.

UK

Andean Trails 72 Newhaven Road, Edinburgh, Scotland EH6 5QG; tel 0131 467 7086; www.andeantrails. co.uk

Andes 37a St Andrew Street, Castle Douglas, Scotland DG7 1EN; tel 01556 503929; www.andes.org.uk

Austral Tours 20 Upper Tachbrook Street, London SW1V 1SH; tel 020 7233 5384; www.latinamerica.co.uk

Exodus Grange Mills, Weir Road, London SW12 0NE; tel 0845 863 9600, tel 020 8772 3936; www.exodus.co.uk

Intrepid Travel 76 Upper Street, Islington, London N1 0NU; tel 020 7354 6169; www.intrepidtravel.com

Journey Latin America 1213 Heathfield Terrace, London W4 4JE; tel 020 8747 8315; www.journeylatinamerica.co.uk

Latin Odyssey 1 Swan Mews, Parsons Green Lane, London SW6 4QT; tel 020 7610 6020; www.latinodyssey.com

Peregrine Adventures 1 Betts Avenue, Martlesham Heath, Ipswich IP5 3RH; tel 0844 736 0170; www.peregrineadventures.com

Pura Aventura 18 Bond Street, Brighton BR1 1RD; tel 0845 225 5058; www.pura-aventura.com

South American Experience Welby House, 96 Wilton Road, London SW1V 1DW; tel 0845 277 3366

Trailfinders 194 Kensington High Street, London W8 6AH; tel 0845 050 5890; www.trailfinders.com

Tucan Travel 316 Uxbridge Road, Acton, London W3 9QP; tel 020 8896 1600; www.tucantravel.com

UNITED STATES

Antares Patagonia 348 Hayes Street, San Francisco, CA 94102; tel 415 703 9955 or 1 800 267 6129 (USA, toll free); www.antarespatagonia.com

Andes Adventures 1323 12th Street, Suite F, Santa Monica, CA 90401; tel 310 395 5265 or 800 289 9470 (USA, toll free); www.andesadventures.com

Aventuras Patagonicas 1303 Sumac Avenue, Boulder, CO 80304; tel 1 888 203 9354 (USA, toll free) or 0800 404 9183 (UK, toll free); www.patagonicas.com

Bio Bio Expeditions PO Box 2028, Truckee, CA 96160; tel 1 530 582 6865, 1 800 246 7238 (USA, toll free) or +56 2 1964 258 (Chile); www.bbxrafting.com

Expediciones Chile PO Box 752, Sun Valley, ID 83353; tel 1 888 488 9082 (USA, toll free); www.exchile.com

Mountain Travel Sobek 1266 66th Street, Suite 4, Emeryville, CA 94608; tel 1 888 831 7526 (USA, toll free); www.mtsobek.com

Sierra Club Outings 85 2nd Street, 2nd Floor, San Francisco, CA 94105; tel 415 977 5522; www.sierraclub.org/outings

Southwind Adventures PO Box 621057, Littleton, CO 80162; tel 800 377 9463 (USA, toll free); www.southwindadventures.com

Wildland Adventures 3516 NE 155th Street, Seattle, WA 98155-7412; tel 206 365 0686 or 800 345 4453 (USA, toll free); www.wildland.com

CHILE

Altue Active Travel General Salvo 159, Providencia, Santiago; tel +56 2 235 1519; www.altue.com

Azimut 360 General Salvo 159, Providencia, Santiago; tel +56 2 235 1519; www.azimut360.com

Cascada Expediciones Don Carlos 3219, Las Condes, Santiago; tel +56 2 232 9878, 0800 051 7095 (UK, toll free) or 1 800 901 6987 (USA, toll free); www.cascada.travel/

Pared Sur Juan Esteban Montero 5497, Las Condes, Santiago; tel +56 2 207 3525; www.paredsur.cl

For tour operators in Puerto Natales, Chile, see Appendix A.

ARGENTINA
Fitz Roy Expediciones San Martín 56, El Chaltén; tel +54 2293 436 424; www.fitzroyexpediciones.com.ar

VISAS AND ARRIVAL

Visas are not required for UK, US and most European nationals travelling to either Chile or Argentina. All foreign visitors are issued with a tourist entry card or *tarjeto de turismo*, valid for 90 days, which must be completed on arrival and presented to border police.

It is important that you keep this entry card, as you will have to present it again on departure from Chile – and failure to do so will make you liable to a fine (roughly US$100), which in some places (including Santiago) is not payable at the airport itself, so you'd probably miss your flight.

If you lose your card, you can get a replacement with little problem (and at no charge) from the Intendencia office of most regional capitals (Santiago: Moneda 1342, tel 02 2672 5320; Punta Arenas: Bories 901, tel 061 2221 675). If you want to stay longer than 90 days, you can extend your entry card once, for a further 90 days, again from the Intendencia office, for about US$100. Alternatively, if you simply head over the border into a neighbouring

Cerro Fitzroy, Los Glaciares national park, Argentina (Walk 8)

country and then return to Chile, you will be issued with a new 90-day tourist entry card for free. Note that on arrival in Chile, US, Canadian and Australian nationals must pay an arrival tax.

Chile operates very strict policies regarding the import of certain foodstuffs into the country. You may not bring in any fresh or dried fruit, nuts or seeds, fresh vegetables, fresh meat or dairy products. Tinned items are allowed, but you'll still need to declare them. You will have to fill out a declaration form on arrival in Chile (at airports and land borders), stating whether or not you are carrying any of the listed foods. If you are carrying any food, or are at all unsure about something, it is much safer to declare it. Bags are checked, and if you are found to be carrying something after not declaring it, you will be fined – which would make a rather bad start to your trip. If you've declared any food you're carrying, there is no fine or penalty if officials find the need to confiscate something.

If any of this seems draconian, consider the Chilean position: agriculture is one of the country's greatest exports, and the arrival of any unwelcome bugs or plant species which would otherwise be unable to cross the Andes, the Pacific, the Atacama or the Southern Ice Sheets would wreak havoc (remember the Carménère grape that survived in Chile but was wiped out by Phylloxera in Europe). Chile has an excellent range of fresh

and dried fruit available, so you really don't need to bring any with you.

ACCOMMODATION

A wide range of accommodation is available in Chile. The various options include *hosterías* (hotels), *hostales* (hostels), *residenciales* (simple, often homely places similar to *pensions*), *hospedajes* (similar to a *residencial*, but usually slightly more low key or basic), *cabañas* (holiday chalets and apartments) and *refugios* (mountain huts). Often there is very little apparent difference between some of the lower- to mid-range *hostales* and *residenciales*; hotels tend to be more expensive than the other types of accommodation. Chilean motels, in contrast to the commonly understood definition of a motel in the UK or US, are places where rooms are usually hired to couples by the hour. Camping is usually permitted only at designated sites. See 'Refugios, campsites and hotels', below, for more information.

LANGUAGE

Chilean Spanish has a number of differences, both in its grammar and vocabulary, from the Castillian Spanish spoken in Spain. It is also spoken at breakneck speed, and contains a fairly hearty dose of slang. So, while you can certainly get by with a smattering of Castillian Spanish, learning a little Chilean Spanish (or other Latin American Spanish) will get you a lot further.

KEY WORDS AND PHRASES FOR TREKKERS	
English	**Chilean Spanish**
bridge	*puente*
campsite	*campamento, camping, zona de acampar*
forest	*bosque*
glacier	*glaciar*
hut	*refugio*
lake	*lago*
mountain	*montaña*
mountain range	*cordillera, sierra*
national park	*parque nacional*
pass	*paso*
path/trail	*sendero*
peak	*cerro, monte*
rain	*lluvia*
river	*río*
tree	*árbol*
warden's office	*guardería*
water	*agua*
wind	*viento*

English is spoken at *refugios*, hotels and hostels, but much less widely than you might expect among taxi drivers, bus drivers and in shops. Many of the words you will encounter in Patagonian Chile – such as the tree name Lenga – are from Mapuche and Tehuelche, local indigenous languages which have otherwise been largely wiped out.

See Appendix C for fuller language notes and glossary.

FOOD AND DRINK

It is hardly surprising, given the length of its coastline, that Chile has an abundant supply of fresh seafood, with excellent dishes ranging from *ceviche*, a marinated fish entrée, to *caldillo de congrio*, a hearty fish stew immortalised in a poem by the Chilean poet Pablo Neruda. Fish is typically cooked *a la plancha*, lightly fried. One of the more commonly found types of fish on restaurant menus is *congrio* (a white-fleshed fish, often mis-translated as conger eel). King crab is a particular speciality of the south, and quite irresistible when prepared as *chupe de centolla* – a fantastically rich sauce cooked with white wine, cream and breadcrumbs.

Red meat is very popular in Chile, in particular beef – usually cooked as an *asado* (often several carcasses splayed out on frames and set around an open fire) or *parilla* (grilled over coals). Another national favourite, *empañadas* (fried or baked filled pastries), make a great snack or entrée. The most traditional variety, the *pino*, contains an olive among the rest of the filling – so watch out for the stone! Chile grows an enormous quantity of fruit and vegetables, so fresh salads are almost always available, as well as staples such as corn and potato, and dried fruit is widley available (perfect for trekking).

Fast food is popular in Chile, in particular huge sandwiches such as the Barros Luco (named after a former Chilean president), containing beef and oozing melted cheese.

Chile produces some outstanding wines, in particular some wonderfully opulent Carménère. The Carménère grape was wiped out in Europe by Phylloxera in the 1860s, but survived in Chile where it had already been imported from France and planted earlier in the 19th century, and it remains the country's signature grape variety. There are a number of vineyards only a short distance from Santiago and Valparaíso offering wine tours (see Appendix A). There are some good locally brewed beers in the south (Austral brewery in Punta Arenas) – and arguably no trip to Chile is complete without sampling that other national beverage, the pisco

sour, an exceptionally drinkable cocktail made from pisco (a spirit made from grapes), lemon, sugar and some frothy egg white.

Coffee, perhaps surprisingly, is often something of a disappointment (in contrast to Argentina), with many restaurants and hotels serving up a decidely watery variety of instant.

A set menu or *menu del día* is almost always cheaper than ordering a la carte, and gets you two or three courses from a couple of options for as little as $5000 (Chilean pesos) or just over £5.

MONEY AND COSTS

The currency in Chile is the peso, properly abbreviated CLP and typically written with a dollar symbol ($) – so fear not, that $1500 *empañada* (filled pastry) is actually only less than £2! Prices in this guide are listed in Chilean pesos, written as $; where prices are quoted in US dollars, they are written as US$. Current exchange rates at the time of writing (2016) are: £1=CLP966, €1=CLP759, US$1=CLP661; CLP1000=£1.04, €1.32 or US$1.51.

Credit cards (Visa and Master Card; Solo and Electron may be less widely accepted) are accepted in larger hotels and restaurants, but typically not in small *hostales* and cheaper places to eat. You can pay by credit card at some of the *refugios* in the national park, but not all of them (and often not for camping). All transport within the park (buses, cata-marans), as well as the park entrance fee itself, needs to be paid in cash – an amount which, you will find, soon adds up (see 'Trekking costs in Torres del Paine national park', below).

There are plenty of ATMs in major towns and cities, including Puerto Natales – but not in Torres del Paine national park or at Cerro Castillo on the bus route in. However, you should not rely on ATMs in Puerto Natales for all the money you need to carry with you in the national park – they frequently run out, keeping (quite reasonably) just enough for locals to use. (Note that when typing in your PIN you will need to chose the *estranjeros* or 'for-eign clients' option.) If you arrived in Puerto Natales on a tight schedule,

only to find you had to wait until 9am the following morning (ie after the bus has left for Torres del Paine) for the ATMs to be refilled, this would effectively delay your start until the afternoon or the following day. So make sure you have enough cash for your time in the park before arriving in Puerto Natales – either by using ATMs in Santiago or Punta Arenas (there's even an ATM at Punta Arenas airport) or buying some Chilean pesos before you travel.

Not all exchange offices in the UK carry Chilean pesos, so ordering in advance is a good idea. (If you're arriving from El Calafate in Argentina and haven't brought Chilean pesos from home, either buy them before getting the bus to Puerto Natales – the rate won't be particulary good though

Low cloud over the Paine massif, from across Lago Pehoé (Walk 1)

SAMPLE PRICES (PER PERSON)	
Double room with shared bathroom in *hostal* (Puerto Natales)	$20,000–$25,000
Bed in *refugio* (Torres del Paine national park)	$30,000–$50,000
Camping (Torres del Paine national park)	$4500–$8500
Bus fare (single, Punta Arenas – Puerto Natales)	$4000
Off-peak Metro ticket (Santiago)	$660
Dinner in *refugio* (Torres del Paine national park)	$12,500
Breakfast in *refugio* (Torres del Paine national park)	$7500
Main course in expensive restaurant (Puerto Natales, Santiago, etc)	$5000
Menu del día (Puerto Natales, Santiago, etc)	$5000
Cup of coffee	$800

– or carry some money in US dollars, euros or pounds sterling which you can change on arrival.)

Trekking costs in Torres del Paine national park

As a rough guide, you will need a minimum of $45,000 (£46, €59, US$68) in cash per person to cover entrance to the park ($18,000), transport to/from the park by bus ($15,000) and the catamaran from Refugio Paine Grande to Pudeto ($12,000), as well as anything from $4500 (£4.65, €6, US$6.80) (camping only) to $26,500 (£27, €35, US$40) (staying in a *refugio*, plus breakfast, lunch and dinner) per person per day, at least partly (if not mostly) in cash.

Even if you camp for your whole time in the national park, the chances are you'll want to order dinner (approx $12,500) and breakfast (approx $7500) from at least some of the *refugios*, to lessen the amount of food that you need to carry. Note that some refugios and campsites now only offer a minimum of full board, which hikes up prices considerably – check when booking.

KEEPING IN TOUCH

The international dialling code for Chile is 56. Area codes relevant to this guide are:
• Santiago   02
• Valparaíso   032
• Puerto Natales and
  Punta Arenas   061

If calling from overseas, omit the first zero of the area code (for example, to call a number in Puerto Natales from the UK, dial 00 56 61 followed by the number; to call the same number from within Chile, dial 061 followed by the number). Chile uses both eight-digit numbers (eg.

The trail above Glaciar Grey (Walk 1)

Santiago) and seven-digit numbers (eg. Puerto Natales).

Calls can be made from phone boxes, using coins or (better) phone cards (*tarjetas telefonicas*) – to phone other countries you'll need to make sure the card covers international calls, *llamadas internacionales*, and not just domestic calls. You can also call from call centres (*centros de llamadas*).

Mobile phones with roaming should work fine in Chile, although many travellers find their mobiles don't work as well as they should, and you may or may not get any reception in the mountains.

The international dialling code for Argentina is 54; the area codes for Buenos Aires, El Calafate and El Chalten are 011, 02902 and 02962 respectively.

Internet cafes are common enough in Chile and Argentina (although the connection can be rather slow) – for internet cafes in Puerto Natales and Punta Arenas see Appendix A.

The postal service is reliable, with post offices (*correos*) on the main square of most towns.

SAFETY

Chile is a fairly safe country in which to travel (although there are a few well-known areas that are less safe after dark, such as the backstreets of Valparaíso), and the author has found Chileans without exception to be uniformly polite, friendly and honest. However you should be aware that, while it may have one of the strongest economies in South America, there is still an enormous gap between rich and poor (as the shantytowns around Santiago clearly show). Carry money in a money belt well hidden beneath your clothing; this should stay hidden, so carry enough money for a couple of days separately rather than delving into it in public.

Whether you carry your passport in a money belt or separately is a matter of choice – if separate, it is more easily accessible at borders and for checking into hotels. You should not assume that fellow travellers are necessarily more honest than locals – never leave items such as passport and camera lying around in a shared room or dorm. It is also prudent to keep a spare copy or photocopy of your air tickets and itinerary, as well as the photo page in your passport.

South American towns often have a fairly large population of stray dogs, and Chile is no exception. Avoid

CHILE AT A GLANCE	
Country name	Republic of Chile
Capital	Santiago
Administrative divisions	15 regions (listed with Roman numerals)
Language	Spanish
Currency	Chilean Peso (CLP, typically written with a dollar sign, $)
Exchange rate	£1=CLP966, €1=CLP759, US$1=CLP661; CLP1000=£1.04, €1.32 or US$1.51.
Population	16,570,000 (2012 census; the methodology used was later called into question)
Land surface area	743,812km^2
Coastline	6435km
Highest point	6891m (Nevado Ojos del Salado)
Time zone	GMT-3 (October–March), GMT-4 (April–September)
International dialling code	+56
Internet country code	.cl
Electricity	220V/50 (two-pin, round rather than flat as in Argentina)
Main religion	Roman Catholicism (70%)
Independence Day (Fiestas Patrias)	18 September

feeding them, whatever sort of eyes they may make at you, or you will be followed relentlessly – including into a national park!

ABOUT THIS GUIDE

This guide contains seven walks in Torres del Paine national park (three of these multi-day treks, and four of them shorter day walks) as well as one (multi-day) trek in Argentina's Los Glaciares national park, and several excursions from Puerto Natales and El Calafate.

Routes are arranged starting with the Torres del Paine Circuit (Walk 1), followed by the half-circuit (Walk 2) and shorter routes in the national park (Walks 3–7); then two other walks within the national park and excursions from Puerto Natales; and the trek in Los Glaciares national park (Walk 8).

Each walk or stage begins with relevant information on transport, accommodation and maps. Difficulty ratings (easy, moderate, difficult) are relative to the other routes in this guide, and are based on terrain, length of stage, cumulative ascent, exposure, any river crossings and so on. They bear no relation to the British adjectival and technical grades for climbing, nor to any other system of climbing or trekking grades.

A reasonable level of fitness is assumed for the longer treks – although they are all technically without difficulty, wind and weather can make them fairly demanding. Timings

refer to walking time only, and do not include time for breaks or stopping at viewpoints and so on. Stages may or may not represent a full day's walking – in some cases, it will be possible to combine two into a single day. Note that in the route descriptions, the term 'true' right/left bank of a river assumes you are looking **downstream**.

The sketch maps in this guide cover all the walks described, and although detailed enough to follow the routes they should ideally be used in conjunction with the CONAF or other maps; all are oriented page north.

CONAF are adamant that only those trails and campsites shown on their 'official' maps should be used by trekkers. Therefore, although a number of other paths are marked on some maps, this guide follows the official version of where you can and cannot trek or camp in Torres del Paine national park. Climbing requires a permit, which can be applied for through DIFROL in Santiago (Teatinos 180 Piso 7, Santiago; tel 02 2827 5900; www.difrol.cl).

Appendix A aims to provide sufficient information on travelling through and staying in the gateway town of Puerto Natales and, to a lesser extent, Santiago and Punta Arenas, without having to carry another guide or guides. Further appendices cover accommodation in Torres del Paine national park, language, contacts, and online resources and further reading.

TREKKING IN TORRES DEL PAINE NATIONAL PARK

Torres del Paine national park is a remote area of wilderness, made surprisingly accessible by clear trails, good public transport and regular huts and campsites. The heart of the Paine Massif consists of vertical peaks of quite spectacular technical difficulty, but the main hiking routes (the 'O' and the 'W') neatly circumnavigate these, giving views from several angles of the national park's most iconic landmarks – the polished, vertical granite Torres ('towers') and craggy, multi-layered Cuernos ('horns'), and the awsome, endless expanse of Glaciar Grey. On two occasions these routes follow valley systems up into the heart of the massif to gain closer vantage points from higher ground, but remain technically straightforward throughout (but see the note on weather conditions below).

The walks in this guide

While it is perfectly feasible to visit some of the more accessible areas of the national park by car, bus or boat, the real way to appreciate Torres del Paine is on foot, ideally by completing one of the two world-class treks the park has to offer, the Torres del Paine Circuit (or 'O', Walk 1) and the half-circuit (the 'W', Walk 2).

The Torres del Paine Circuit includes side trips to the 'towers' and the Valle Francés, passing beneath the 'horns' and crossing Paso John Gardner, with the awe-inspiring expanse of the Glaciar Grey sprawled below. The shorter 'W' follows the southern section of the Circuit, taking in many – but not all – of the longer route's highlights, and is the busier of the two. You should figure on roughly 10 to 11 days to walk the Circuit – more if you are unable to cross Paso John Gardner due to bad weather – and 4 to 5 days for the 'W'.

Both of these routes can be walked in either direction. However, for the Circuit, you are better off going anticlockwise (as described in this guide), since this will give you the most impressive views from the John Gardner pass (and they really are impressive). Walk 1 is a slightly longer variation of the official route of the Circuit, as it includes a walk-in from the CONAF Administración office at Lago Toro (which effectively turns the route into the shape of a reversed 'Q') – definitely the most impressive way to start the route. The 'W' is described from east to west, starting from Refugio Las Torres, although it could just as easily be walked the other way, from Refugio Paine Grande. Decide this based on the weather – particularly, when you are most likely to have clear views of the 'towers' from Mirador Las Torres.

For both routes, the various possible starting points are accessible by public transport from Puerto Natales – by bus to the CONAF Administración office on Lago Toro (the start of Walk 1); the same bus to Pudeto followed by a catamaran to Refugio Paine

Peaks above Glaciar Grey (Walks 1 and 2)

Grande (a popular start/finish point for both the 'O' and the 'W'); or the same bus to the CONAF office at Laguna Amarga, followed by a shuttle bus to Refugio Las Torres (the start of Walk 2 as it is described here).

While both walks are technically straightforward, you should never underestimate the Patagonian climate, which can be fickle indeed. Gale-force winds can make it almost impossible – or at least, extremely dangerous – for trekkers to cross the John Gardner pass, while streams and rivers can flood, bridges become submerged, forest trails turn into mud slurries and temperatures plummet. At the same time thick, low cloud can roll in and completely obscure what might otherwise be considered a perfectly clear route – not to mention that view you've

come half way around the world to see. So, when planning your trek, you will need to factor in an extra day or two in case of bad weather.

Both the Circuit and the 'W' have very clear trails and only moderate ascent/descent, the exceptions being the hike up to Mirador Las Torres (Walks 1 and 2) and crossing Paso John Gardner (Walk 1), each of which involves several hundred metres of ascent/descent.

There are a fair number of river crossings on the two walks, mostly by bridges, but (particularly on the northern section of the Circuit) sometimes by way of a shallow (perfectly easy) ford. However, after heavy rain rivers can swell considerably and some of the low bridges become submerged, and under such conditions you need to evaluate the situation and cross with care (link arms and use sticks or walking poles for additional balance, and be careful of boulders being shifted along the bottom by the current).

The walks are described in stages that are usually, although not always, a full day's walking, and always finish at a hut/campsite. Some of the shorter stages, usually side trips from the main route, can be combined into a single day. There are campsites (sometimes serviced, sometimes unserviced) on every stage of Walks 1 and 2. It is also possible to stay in huts for many stages of Walk 1, and all except one of Walk 2 (although you can get round this, if you don't want to camp, by shortening the preceding stage); for the rest of the time, you'll need to camp. So, unless you're on an organized trek, you'll need to carry a tent and sleeping bag, as well as food and a stove for at least some of the stages – although when staying at or camping by a hut (and there are campsites by all the huts), you can order meals there.

There are also some shorter, less well-known walks in the national park, most of which see far fewer people than the main hiking trails, and which range in length from 2 to 3 days (Walk 7, Río Pingo and Mirador Zapata) to a couple of hours (Walk 3, Salto Grande and Mirador Los Cuernos).

While staying in Puerto Natales and El Calafate, there are also some very worthwhile excursions (described in this guide) – the Balmaceda glacier

from the former and the Perito Moreno glacier from the latter, for example – which may or may not involve much actual walking (the Balmaceda glacier is accessible only by boat, and the trip includes scope for only a 15min walk, but it's a magnificent excursion).

The entry fee for Torres del Paine national park is $18,000 (reduced during the winter), payable on arrival (and in cash) at Laguna Amarga, where the bus from Puerto Natales will stop for this purpose. The ticket is supposed to be single entry, although in practice you are unlikely to stray out of the park (unless perhaps at Laguna Verde). In any case, keep your entry tickets with you. You will also be given the small CONAF map, which is perfectly acceptable for hiking (see 'Maps', below).

REFUGIOS, CAMPSITES AND HOTELS

A network of huts in the national park covers most, though not all, of the main hiking routes; for those sections without a hut, there are campsites. On the 'W' you no longer need to camp at all. For the Circuit, you will need to camp at three more sites, in addition to those mentioned for the 'W'.

You can also camp at the *refugios* on all the other stages, thus keeping costs down while making the most of the meals available in the huts, and reducing the amount of food (and fuel) you need to carry. Meals can be ordered at *refugios* regardless of whether you are staying in them, camping, or just passing by.

One major new regulation in Torres del Paine, introduced at the end of 2016, is that **pre-booking accommodation on the Circuit and the 'W' is mandatory**. This includes all the refugios and campsites run by Fantastico Sur and Vertice, and in January/February you also need to pre-book the free CONAF-run campsites. Proof of bookings is checked at the national park entrance, as well as at huts and guarderias along the route. Furthermore, you can now only stay at each of the various refugios and campsites for one day, before moving on.

Facilities at campsites vary – showers and toilets when adjacent to a hut; unserviced (toilet only) when not. In the latter case they are usually (not always) free, although there is a charge for the campsites next to huts. Wild camping in the national park is strictly prohibited. The larger huts, such as Refugio Paine Grande and Refugio Las Torres, have their own bedding; the smaller ones, like Refugio El Chileno, do not, so you will need your own sleeping bag (or these will usually be available for hire).

You should consider booking a place at huts (the same goes for any equipment/bedding hire) in advance where possible, particularly in summer. All the *refugios* are run by two companies, Fantástico Sur and Vertice (see Appendix B for information on all accommodation in the national park), and staff can book your next

Welcome sign at Refugio Dickson (Walk 1)

night ahead. Increasingly, this is also the case with campsites, in particular on the 'W' (ie Campamento Italiano) in January/February. Unless otherwise specified, expect to pay around $4500 per person camping, and from $30,000 for a bed in a *refugio*.

There are also a number of upmarket hotels (*hosterías*) in the national park, although only one of them is actually on the Circuit and all are expensive and, frankly, an eyesore. There is also the option of staying in large, comfortable geodomes (dome-shaped, tent-like dwellings, such as those at EcoCamp Patagonia).

TRANSPORT TO AND AROUND THE PARK

There are regular **bus** services from Puerto Natales to the national park, stopping at Laguna Amarga, where you buy park entry tickets. Here you can change to a shuttle bus for nearby Refugio Las Torres – an additional $2500 – or walk into the park. The bus then continues to Pudeto (for the catamaran service to Refugio Paine Grande – see below for more information) and Administración (CONAF Administration Office, the starting point for Walk 1), near Lago Toro. You

Bus Timetables Puerto Natales – Torres del Paine		
Buses Gomez and Buses Pacheco		
Puerto Natales	0730	1430
Laguna Amarga	0945	1630
Pudeto	1045	1730
Administración	1145	1800
Administración	1300	1815
Pudeto	1330 (Pacheco)	1900
	1345 (Gomez)	1900
Laguna Amarga	1500	1945
Puerto Natales	1700	2145
Bus-Sur		
Puerto Natales	0730	1430
Laguna Amarga	0945	1630
Pudeto	1045	1730
Administración	1145	1800
Administración	1300	1800
Pudeto	1330	1900
Laguna Amarga	1430	1945
Puerto Natales	1630	2145
Shuttle service Refugio Las Torres – Laguna Amarga		
Connecting with services to Administración	0900	1600
Connecting with services to Puerto Natales	1400	1900
Details correct at time of going to press in 2013		

Catamaran Timetable Pudeto – Refugio Paine Grande			
16 November – 15 March			
from Pudeto	0925	1155	1755
From Refugio Paine Grande	0955	1225	1825
16 March – 15 November (*16 March – 31 March only)			
From Pudeto	1155	1755*	
From Refugio Paine Grande	1225	1825*	
Details correct at time of going to press in 2016			

can also usually ask to be dropped off at other points.

Several companies run services on this route, Buses Gomez (Arturo Prat 234; tel 061 2411 971; www.busesgomez.com), Buses Pacheco (Ramirez 224; tel 061 2414 800; www.busespacheco.com) and Bus-Sur (Baquedano 668; tel 061 2614 220; www.bussur.cl); note that if you buy a return ticket you will have to return with the same company. Tickets (single/return) cost around $8000/$15,000 (Puerto Natales – Administración); single fares between any points in the park (for example Administración and Pudeto) are $2000. Buses for Torres del Paine pick up in Puerto Natales outside the bus companies' offices on Arturo Prat, near the corner of the Plaza (see Appendix A).

A **catamaran** service runs between Pudeto and Refugio Paine Grande (subject to weather conditions), taking about 25mins. Tickets are $12,000 ($19,000 return), and you have to pay in cash. A supplement is usually charged if you're carrying more than one pack per person. The service runs between mid-November and mid-March, with a reduced service for a couple of additional weeks either side of this.

MAPS

The map 'CONAF Parque Nacional Torres del Paine', given free when you pay your park entry fee at Laguna Amarga or the administration office (CONAF Administración) by Lago Toro, is perfectly adequate for trekking in the national park (and is the recommended map for routes in this guide within the park). There is no scale, annoyingly (although it works out at roughly 1:130,000), but it has almost as much detail as any of the slightly larger maps listed below (including 250m contour lines), and has the advantage of being smaller and lighter. The fact that it is produced by CONAF should also mean that it's the most accurate available – although this is not always entirely so. It is worth pointing out that this is not necessarily the map you'll see, enlarged, at the reception desk of some huts.

Also widely available is 'Torres del Paine Trekking Map' (Mapas sheet 13, 1:100,000, 25m contour lines), which covers a larger area than the CONAF map, from the Balmaceda glacier and the head of Seno Ultima Esperanza in the south to Lago Dickson in the north. This is on balance the best map commercially available, and if you feel the need to buy a larger and slightly more detailed map than the free CONAF one, this is the one to go for. Another 'Torres del Paine Trekking Map' (Zagier & Urruty, 1:80,000) is simply a larger and bulkier version – in this case, a satellite view with some contour lines. A useful map for planning other excursions in the area is 'Puerto Natales Calafate' (Mapas sheet 21, 1:500,000), which includes

the whole area from Puerto Natales to El Calafate. The Mapas sheets have various bits of fairly useful information on the back. None of these maps (including the CONAF one) is without its inaccuracies, however – including non-existent *hosterías* and campsites, and questionable hiking trails.

Chile is also covered by a series of military maps (IGM).

Good map shops in the UK include The Map Shop (15 High Street, Upton Upon Severn; tel 01684 593 146; www.themapshop.co.uk) and Stanfords (12–14 Long Acre, London; tel 020 7836 1321; www.stanfords.co.uk).

EQUIPMENT

If you walk the Circuit you will be carrying your equipment for quite some time, and careful thought of what to take and what to leave behind will

Flooded trail between Refugio Las Torres and Campamento Serón (Walk 1)

make a great difference to your enjoyment of the trek. Even for day trips, you will still need to carry adequate warm clothing and wet-weather gear, as listed below.

Wet-weather gear is mandatory – if you get round the whole trek without getting rained on, count yourself lucky indeed. Tents should be wind-cheating designs, either tunnel or dome, and able to withstand strong winds. There are many river crossings on the trek, most of them with bridges but plenty more without. Since you will therefore be doing a fair amount of wading, a decent pair of rafting or trekking sandals will make life much more comfortable.

One thing you'll see quite a lot of on the Circuit or the 'W' is

EQUIPMENT CHECKLIST

- Rucksack (approximately 60–80 litres capacity)
- Walking boots, with Vibram soles (wear them in before your trip)
- Rafting or trekking sandals, such as those made by Keen (for river crossings and towns)
- Rainproof, breathable shell (Gore Tex, eVENT or similar material)
- Warm, preferably windproof fleece (Polartec or similar material) jacket or mid-layer
- Light thermal base layer
- Long trousers (lightweight, quick-drying material), long-sleeved shirt, T-shirts, underwear
- Good quality walking socks (these counter the need to wear two layers of socks or sock-liners)
- Warm gloves and hat
- Sleeping bag (three-season will be fine for summer use)
- Sleeping mat (closed cell or inflatable)
- Reliable tent, able to stand up to extremely strong winds
- Water bottles (lightweight aluminium and/or collapsible plastic bladders)
- Stove (preferably multi-fuel such as MSR) and compatible fuel bottle(s)
- Lightweight cooking pot, fork and spoon
- Compass and relevant maps (and the knowledge of how to use them)
- Torch (headtorches are best)
- Sunglasses and sun-block
- Biodegradable soap
- Small first-aid kit
- Swiss army knife
- Whistle (for attracting attention in an emergency)

- Walking poles
- Emergency reflective bag or 'space blanket'
- Matches (keep them dry in a plastic bag)
- Large plastic rucksack liner
- Mosquito repellent (especially during January/February)
- Small two-pin adaptor (220V/50HZ)
- Adequate food
- Camera, memory cards or film, batteries and charger

In addition to the above, you may wish to add:
- Lightweight day pack
- Down jacket (it can get remarkably chilly on that pre-dawn hike up to the towers)
- Small water filter such as Sawyer Mini

rucksack covers, usually hired with other equipment. My advice is not to bother with these – they simply serve as something for the Patagonian wind to get under and try and blow off you. Instead, waterproof your gear from inside your pack by putting everything in heavy-duty plastic bags and a pack liner or dustbin liner (or use waterproof stuff sacks).

Some equipment can be hired in Puerto Natales or at *refugios* in the park (and you can buy some equipment in Puerto Natales) – although what you get may not be as light or compact as gear available in the UK (the best place to hire gear in Puerto Natales is Erratic Rock, see Appendix A). Unless hiking is not your main reason for visiting Chile, bring your own gear from home.

Despite the fact that some equipment can be hired in Chile, one thing you're extremely unlikely to be able to replace is your hiking boots. So, allowing that baggage does very occasionally get lost on flights (whether to Chile or anywhere else in the world), wear your boots on the plane.

Trail food

In Chile you can easily stock up on trail food – dried fruit and nuts, quince paste, pumpernickel bread or similar (which won't go stale or mouldy), cheeses and dried meat are all readily available in supermarkets.

LOW-IMPACT TREKKING

Torres del Paine regularly attracts over 140,000 visitors per year, the vast majority of them in the main trekking season. Such a large number of visitors inevitably places a strain on the park ecologically, from trail erosion to waste management.

Unfortunately the maintenance of the park is not always up to a standard you might expect of such a popular area. Wooden boardwalks remain incomplete in places, marker poles are often just grey plastic pipes with a piece of orange plastic attached, and by the late summer toilets at campsites can be filthy.

To minimise your environmental impact, please keep to the following principles.

- **Stick to established trails**
  Walking to either side of an established trail simply widens it, increases erosion and damages surrounding plant life. As an example, Balsam Bog or *Llareta* (*Bolax gummifer*) appears a hardy enough plant but takes approximately 10 years to recover from a single human boot-print. Please stick to marked trails and don't take shortcuts. Occasionally trails are clearly diverted to let an area recover; please follow these diversions.

- **Never light open fires**
  Fire is a constant threat. In 2005 a fire broke out near Laguna Azul when a camp stove was accidentally knocked over. Fanned by winds it spread quickly, raging for over a month and consuming an area of some 150km^2 before firefighters could finally bring it under control. In 2011 another fire destroyed over 85km^2 in the south of the park.

- **Carry all litter out of the park**
  Yes, some *refugios* have litter bins, and yes, someone else will collect and empty them; but in the meantime your litter could be blown off by the wind or dragged

Sign on the trail to Cerro Torre, Los Glaciares national park (Walk 8)

Quemar papel higiénico provoca Incendios
Burning toilet paper causes Forest Fires

Refugio Paine Grande (Walks 1 and 2)

away by wildlife. Take all your litter out of the park (after all, it doesn't weigh much by that stage) and dispose of it sensibly in a town.

- **Camp only at designated sites**
  Wild camping is strictly prohibited in the national park, and you face a hefty fine if you're caught.

- **Use toilets at huts and campsites**
  It takes several months for toilet paper to fully decompose; use the toilets at huts and campsites, otherwise always bury toilet waste 6 inches underground. Do **not** burn toilet paper.

- **Do not contaminate streams**
  Use biodegradable soap and avoid washing dishes, or yourself, directly in streams and rivers.

- **Don't buy bottled water**
  Take a filter or purifying tablets. While this means either additional weight or less pleasant tasting water, bottles create waste

– not all of which is going to be recycled.

- **Buy local produce where possible**
  Chile grows a wonderful variety of fruit and vegetables, and as you won't be allowed to bring dried fruit and nuts into the country, you should make the most of what's available locally. In doing so, you will support small businesses and the local economy. In Puerto Natales there's an excellent little shop selling dried fruit and nuts – perfect for stocking up before your trek (see Appendix A).

- **Think about where you stay**
  Over the years a number of large, luxury hotels have sprung up in the national park. The regulation of development within Chilean national parks such as Torres del Paine compares unfavourably with the situation in Los Glaciares national park in neighbouring

Argentina, where no construction whatsoever has been allowed. Visitors there simply have the choice between staying in El Chaltén and exploring the national park as day trips, or camping at designated sites. It seems fair to say that creating further visitor demand for these hotels (which then expand further) in Torres del Paine does little positive for the environment of this national park.

For further information on minimizing your impact on the environment while hiking in Torres del Paine or elsewhere, see the Leave No Trace Centre for Outdoor Ethics website (www.lnt.org).

WHAT TO DO IN AN EMERGENCY

All those venturing into the mountains should be aware of the possible dangers, be prepared to administer basic first aid, and know how to react in an emergency. Always observe the following basic precautions.

- Leave your itinerary with someone at home.
- Where possible, give details of your plans for the day to a hut warden, locals or other walkers.
- Do not set off on high or exposed routes in bad weather.
- Always carry adequate warm and waterproof clothing.
- Always carry an adequate supply of food and water, remembering that if you get stuck, you will need a little extra.
- Always carry a compass and the relevant map(s) – and know how to use them.
- Always carry a small first-aid kit and an emergency bag or 'space blanket', a torch and a small whistle for attracting attention.

These signals are used to communicate with a helicopter.

help needed

raise both arms above head to form a 'V'

help not needed

raise one arm above head, extend other arm downward

Emergency telephone numbers:

Air rescue	138
Ambulance	131
Police (carabineros)	133

- Learn to recognize the symptoms of exposure or hypothermia – numbness in hands and feet, shivering, loss of coordination, slurred speech, shallow breathing, impaired vision. Get the victim out of wind or rain, replace wet clothing with warm, dry garments, and give hot fluids and foods with high sugar and carbohydrate levels.
- Know the internationally recognized call for help: six visual or audible signals (torch, whistle, etc) per minute, followed by a minute's pause, then repeated. The answer is three signals per minute followed by a minute's pause.
- Know the emergency signals to rescue helicopters: both arms raised above the head means YES, help required; one arm raised above the head with the other extended downwards means NO, help not required.
- Finally, make sure your chosen insurance policy covers accidents in the mountains (many don't).

In the event of an emergency while hiking in Torres del Paine national park, contact the nearest *guardería* (ranger station) – easiest to do by tele-phoning the nearest hut. Some of the huts have public telephones.

Several new regulations intended to reduce overcrowding on the trails came into effect at the end of 2016, which have a major impact on how you plan your trek in Torres del Paine national park:

- Trekkers must now book all accommodation in advance. This includes all the refugios and campsites run by Fantastico Sur and Vertice, and in January/February you also need to pre-book free campsites. Proof of bookings is checked at the national park entrance.
- The Circuit (Walk 1) can now only be walked anticlockwise (as described in this guide).
- During high season, the CONAF Administración on Lago Toro can no longer be used as an entry to the park, only an exit, meaning that the first stage of Walk 1, arguably the most pleasant way to begin your trek, is no longer possible in January/February. (It would still be possible to walk it in reverse, as a way out after completing the Circuit). Campamento Las Carretas on this stage is also now closed.
- Campamento Torres in the Valle Ascencio, for a long time the base for pre-dawn ascents to Mirador Las Torres, is closed. This means that to see the towers at dawn you need to stay at Refugio el Chileno and start your ascent at least 1hr 15mins earlier.
- Further new regulations may be introduced, so check for any other changes that would affect your planned route when booking accommodation.

TORRES DEL PAINE
NATIONAL PARK, CHILE

The Cuernos del Paine viewed across Lago Pehoé (Walk 1)

WALK 1
Torres del Paine Circuit (the 'O')

Peaks above Glaciar Grey, Torres del Paine national park

The Torres del Paine Circuit, also known as the 'O', is a circular route through the national park, taking in many of its scenic highlights. An extended trek through remote, ever-changing and often spectacular mountain scenery, it is without doubt the finest walk in the park, and one of the world's truly great treks. The route includes side trips to the 'towers' and the sublimely beautiful Valle Francés, and passes beneath the iconic Cuernos ('horns') del Paine as well as above and alongside the awe-inspiring expanse of the Grey glacier, and through beautiful forests of Megallenic Coigüe, Antarctic Beech and *Lenga*. Although not technically difficult, it is a fairly committing undertaking – there's no convenient exit point halfway through. The highest point on the Circuit, Paso John Gardner, is only 1180m, but the wind can make it almost impossible to stand up.

While the Circuit can be walked in either direction, following the route anticlockwise – as described here – will give you the most impressive views from Paso John Gardner. The route includes a walk-in to Refugio Paine Grande from the CONAF Administración office on Lago

Start/Finish	CONAF Administración (Lago Toro)/Refugio Paine Grande
Distance	140.5km
Duration	10 to 11 days for the route as described here (some of the stages can be combined into a single day), but longer if bad weather prevents a crossing of Paso John Gardner.
Maps	See sketch maps and the CONAF map given free when paying your entrance fee to the national park.
Transport	Take the bus from Puerto Natales to the CONAF Administración office on Lago Toro (the last stop). If you want to start from Refugio Paine Grande, get off the bus at Pudeto and take the catamaran from there; for Refugio Las Torres, get off the bus at Laguna Amarga and take the shuttle (or walk, see below) to Refugio Las Torres.
Accommodation	Huts are an option for most, but not all stages, otherwise there is a mixture of serviced/unserviced campsites. Camping is the only option at Stages 2/3 (Campamento Italiano), Stages 5/6 (El Chileno), Stage 9 (Campamento Serón) and Stages 11/12 (Campamento Los Perros, Campamento Paso). Further accommodation options include EcoCamp Patagonia and Hotel Las Torres (Stage 4) and Posada Río Serrano (Stage 1). Meals are available from huts, whether you're camping or staying in a room. Refugio Paine Grande is marked as Refugio Pehoé on some maps. See Appendix B for a full list of huts, campsites and other accommodation options.
Note	At present, this can't be walked in January and February.

Toro, rather than taking the catamaran from Pudeto to the *refugio*, a variant which turns the walk from an 'O' into a reversed 'Q' shape, so to speak.

Alternative start: walking from Laguna Amarga ticket office to Refugio Las Torres

If you wish to start the Circuit from Refugio Las Torres, it's possible (and arguably more pleasant) to walk there from Laguna Amarga, rather than taking the shuttle bus. Allow just over 1hr.

From the ticket office turn right and follow the road downhill to the narrow bridge (passengers in the shuttle bus have to get out here and walk anyway). After the bridge, take the path on the left, cross a small stream and ascend to rejoin the road. Follow the road, with views of the 'towers' ahead, and pass through the gate to Estancia Paine – this part of the national park is still private land – before rounding a corner and descending to reach Refugio las Torres.

Short walks from CONAF Administración

There are fine views of the Cuernos from the Administración. Just walk over the road and up the bank beside the old cottages, 2mins away. If you arrive early at the Administración and have a little spare time, consider hiking back along the road to the Weber Bridge (Puente Weber, see Walk 4) or further to Mirador Lago Toro (see Walk 5).

STAGE 1

CONAF Administración – Refugio Paine Grande

Start	CONAF Administración
Distance	17.5km
Rating	easy–moderate
Time	5hrs 45mins
Maximum altitude	200m
Map	CONAF Parque Nacional Torres del Paine
Accommodation	Refugio Paine Grande (Vertice, tel 061 2412 742 or 061 2415 693, www.verticepatagonia.com). If you arrive very late at the CONAF office and need to camp, ask politely at the office and you may be allowed to pitch a tent on the level, grassy area behind the building. Camping Río Serrano (www.horseridingpatagonia.com), about 6km S of here, will pick guests up from the CONAF office.

This stage provides an alternative walk-in to Refugio Paine Grade, rather than taking the catamaran from

Pudeto, and provides excellent views of the Paine Massif opening up before you. However, as of the 2016/17 season trekkers can no longer use the CONAF Administración on Lago Toro as an entry to the park during high season, only as an exit; meaning that it is currently not possible to walk this stage in the direction described in January/February (and the restriction may be extended to cover a longer period), although it would still be possible to walk it in reverse, ie as a way out after completing the circuit or W. Check the status when booking your accommodation; you may have to get the catamaran from Pudeto to Refugio Paine Grande and begin your trek there.

The **CONAF administration office** (Sede Administrativa, or just Administración) is open 8.30am–7pm, 7 days a week including holidays. There is a small gazebo out over the water, with lovely views across Lago Toro, and some well-preserved old colonial-style wooden houses just across the road. The bus to Laguna Amarga and Puerto Natales picks up and drops off passengers directly outside the office.

From in front of the **CONAF Administración**, walk left onto the road, then right at the intersection (marked 'Hostería Lago Grey'). After a few minutes, at a marker pole and a road sign ('Administración 10km'), turn right onto a trail with marker poles, heading W then NW. Head away from the road, over a slight rise, with glimpses of a spiky peak ahead and an expansive view of the Cuernos opening up on the right, before being obscured by a low ridge. The slopes of the ridge are covered with large, brain-shaped plants, which on closer inspection prove to be spiky green bushes. This is Mata Barrosa (*Mulinum spinosum*), which will be a familiar sight in the days to come. Equally familiar will be the shattered and bleached-looking trees up on the ridge. Continue over windswept grasslands, the trail at times broadening into a 4WD track, to arrive at

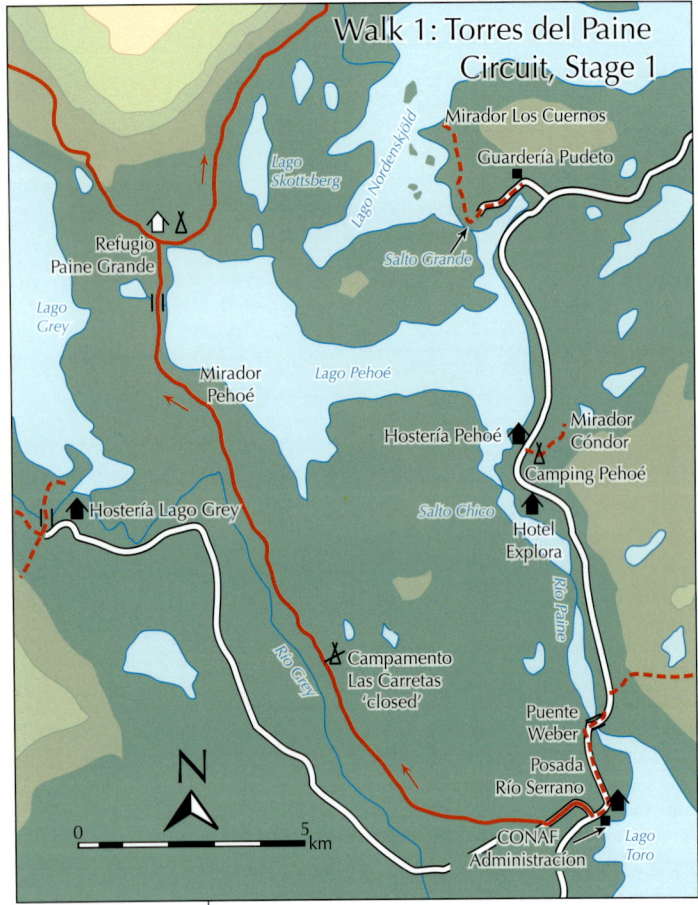

Campamento Las Carretas (now closed – camping prohibited), 2hrs 30mins from the CONAF Administración.

Continue from Campamento Las Carretas, coming close to the true left bank of Río Grey and passing alongside shattered, weather-bleached trees. Pass a marshy area on your right, then ascend over an eroded bluff. Descend,

The trail alongside Río Grey

passing more marshy areas on your right and left. The view ahead is dominated by the bristling form of Cerro Paine Grande, and that to the W across the Río Grey by Cerro Ferrier. The road on the other side of the river leads to Hostería Lago Grey and the start of the Río Pingo trek (Walk 7). Looking back the way you've come (SSE) you'll see the distinctive, cone-like form of Cerro Tenerife.

Carry on alongside the Río Grey, then ascend away from it to the right onto open, level pastures with occasional marker poles. Just over 2hrs from Campamento Las Carretas, you arrive at a sign and lookout point on your right, **Mirador Pehoé**. From here you get your first breathtaking view of the Cuernos and Cerro Paine Grande across Lago Pehoé. The lake can be an intense blue or turquoise, the result of glacial sediment carried down by mountain streams.

Walk alongside Lago Pehoé, first ascending (excellent views from here) then descending again through *Notro* or Firebushes and crossing a low bridge over a broad river running into the lake from the W. (After heavy rain both ends of the bridge are likely to be under water, in which case you will have to wade carefully –up

The Cuernos viewed across Lago Pehoé

to knee deep – using walking poles and following the path to reach the bridge.) This is a good area for spotting Neotropic Cormorant (*Phalacrocorax brasilianus*, known locally as Yeco) and Great Grebe (*Podiceps major*, known locally as *Huala*). Ascend again, with more wonderful views, before descending finally (slightly exposed, and just above the point where the catamaran departs for Pudeto) to **Refugio Paine Grande**.

Refugio Paine Grande is a wonderful place to stop, with a spacious lodge and good meals served in the large, busy restaurant (you will no doubt appreciate the generous portions even more when you arrive here after completing the Circuit). There's even a small (but noisy) bar upstairs. Campsites are scattered behind and E of the lodge (where it tends to be quieter). Try to choose a site in the lee of the thick bushes, as the wind from the N can be quite strong.

The camping office is around the back of the lodge, by the small minimarket. The minimarket is, not surprisingly, quite expensive, but is the last decent place to stock up for the whole trek (that includes Refugio Las

Torres, which is far less well supplied), and sells bread, pasta, dried fruit, soups, salami and chocolate, among other things. Wooden boardwalks lead from behind the lodge to toilets and showers, and there's also a pleasant little wooden *quincho* – a small pavilion which functions as a communal dining area. The restaurant serves dinner 7–8pm, breakfast 7.30–9am, and lunch 12am–2pm.

STAGE 2

Refugio Paine Grande – Campamento Italiano

Start	Refugio Paine Grande
Distance	7.5km
Rating	easy
Time	2hrs 30mins
Maximum altitude	200m
Map	CONAF Parque Nacional Torres del Paine; **note** some maps mark Valle Francés as Valle del Francés
Accommodation	Refugio Paine Grande (Vertice, tel 061 2412 742 or 061 2415 693, www.verticepatagonia.com); Campamento Italiano, Camp Francés

A short, easy stage, which should leave you plenty of time to complete the return-hike up the Valle Francés (Stage 3) the same day. If Campmento Italiano is full, the nearest campsite is Camp Francés.

From **Refugio Paine Grande** head E past the *guardería* (warden's office), ascending and crossing a stream. The trail then veers left, with good views ahead to the Cuernos and Cerro Espada. It can get quite windy along this section.

Continue above **Lago Skottsberg**, then along sections of wooden boardwalk. Pass a sign reading 'bridge 500m', then after crossing a small bridge reach a longer bridge over the Río Francés. Cross one person at a time

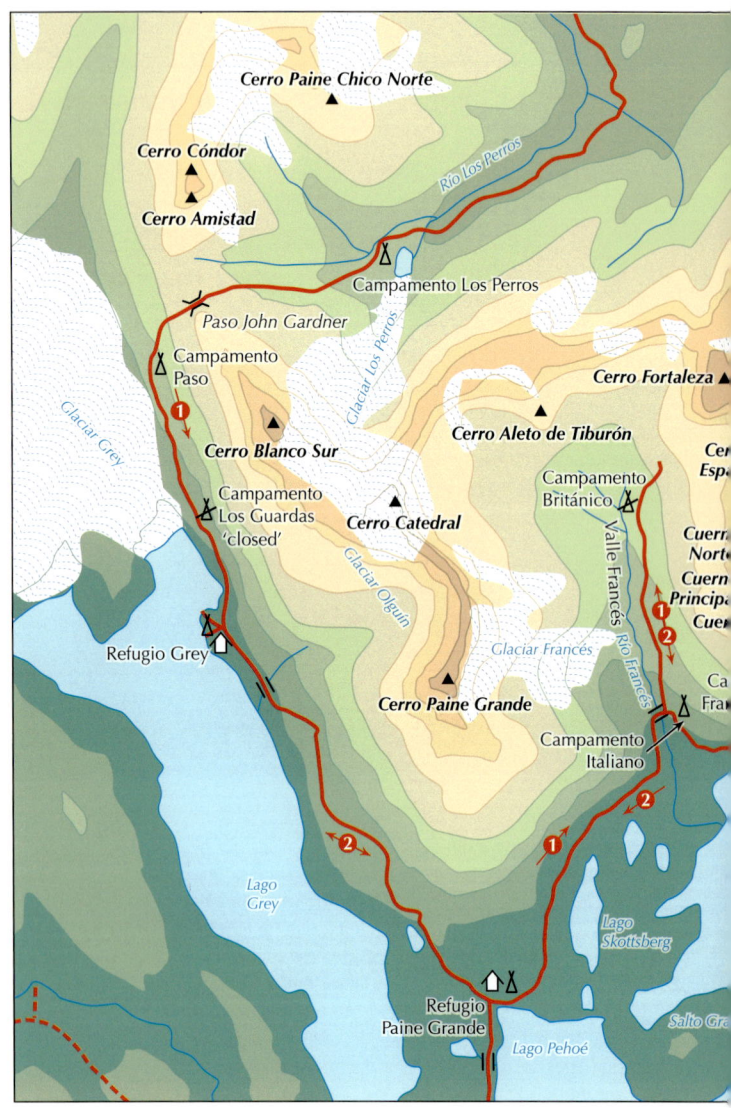

Walk 1: Torres del Paine Circuit, Stages 2–8
Walk 2: Torres del Paine half-circuit

Fortaleza, Cerro Espada and the Cuernos del Paine

to arrive at **Campamento Italiano**. Do not try to ford the river under any circumstances.

Campamento Italiano lies scattered along the riverbank, sheltered among the trees. The *guardería* and larger camping area are on the left (upstream); the quieter campsites tend to be those on the right (downstream), but so is the toilet. Camping here is free. There are excellent views of the E face of Cerro Paine Grande from the open, boulder-strewn area by the river.

STAGE 3
Campamento Italiano – Valle Francés (return)

Start	Campamento Italiano
Distance	13km
Rating	moderate
Time	5hrs (return)
Maximum altitude	835m
Map	CONAF Parque Nacional Torres del Paine
Accommodation	Campamento Italiano

Although not as well known or photographed as the 'towers' and 'horns', the Valle Francés is one of the most beautiful areas in the park. This short excursion up the valley and back can easily be combined with the walk from Refugio Paine Grande (Stage 2) on the same day. Alternatively, Valle Francés would make an exceptionally pleasant spot to spend a rest day – although the campsite up towards the head of the valley, Campamento Británico, has now been closed.

Head N from **Campamento Italiano**, following the true left bank of the Río Francés and climbing gradually. As you gain height there are stupendous views of the huge E face of Cerro Paine Grande, with the Glaciar Francés sprawling below.

Cross a side-stream after 30mins, just below a waterfall, then pass a large stream to reach a clearing with wind-blasted tree stumps and wonderful views back over the intense turquoise of Lago Nordenskjöld. Carry on, crossing minor streams to reach a large rocky clearing (good views of Cerro Fortaleza on the right, as well as the 'back' of the Cuernos), before arriving at the old **Campamento Británico**, hidden in the trees on the other side of the river, 2hrs 30mins from Campamento Italiano.

Campamento Británico used to provide a basic, quieter alternative to Camapamento Italiano, but has been closed since the first edition of this guide. It was from this base that a British team climbed Cerro Fortaleza in 1968.

Continue from Campamento Británico, climbing gradually, with the huge panorama of peaks at the head of Valle Francés opening up before you, to reach the mirador (viewpoint) in 20mins. This is little more than a small rock outcrop, and the views from it not that much better than those 5mins below it; but it's a wonderful spot nonetheless, with one of the finest views in the national

The amphitheatre of peaks at the head of Valle Francés

park. The prominent, fin-like peak is Cerro Aleto de Tiburón ('shark's fin').

Descend to **Campamento Italiano** by the same route.

STAGE 4
Campamento Italiano – Refugio Las Torres

Start	Campamento Italiano
Distance	16.5km
Rating	easy–moderate
Time	6hrs 15mins
Maximum altitude	235m
Map	CONAF Parque Nacional Torres del Paine
Accommodation	Camping/Domos Francés; Refugio Los Cuernos; Refugio Las Torres; Refugio El Chileno (all run by Fantastico Sur, tel 061 2614 184, www.fantasticosur.com); EcoCamp Patagonia (tel 02 2923 5950 or 0800 051 7095 (toll free from UK), www.ecocamp.travel); Hotel Las Torres (tel 061 2617 450 or 061 2617 451, www.lastorres.com)

A rather longer day than it looks on the map, but with beautiful views across Lago Nordenskjöld.

From **Campamento Italiano**, follow the trail SE, passing a sign warning (for the benefit of those walking in the opposite direction) 'Do not ford river'. Follow wooden boardwalks, descending slightly and passing through a small clearing, crossing a bridge over a small stream to reach the new Camp Francés/Domos Francés, with its cluster of geo-domes. Ascend again, to reach a lookout 45mins from camp. Descend, and follow the shore of Lago Nordenskjöld, walking alongside pebble beaches with views across to rolling hills on its S shore – a pleasant spot to linger. Ascend slightly before walking through sheltered tent sites to reach **Refugio Los Cuernos**.

Refugio Los Cuernos (also known as Albergo Los Cuernos) has beds in the hut as well as in several small cabins, and camping among the bushes nearby. It serves breakfast, lunch and dinner.

View across Lago Nordenskjöld

Continue, crossing a bridge over a stream and ascending to reach a shoulder with good views, 1hr from Refugio Los Cuernos. There are glimpses of the entrance to the Valle Bader above you on your left, beside the distinctive form of the eastern 'horn' (Cuerno Este). Descend fairly steeply before fording a succession of streams, the first of these reasonably large. Care is needed here after heavy rain. Ascend slightly, passing a sign reading 'Hostería Las Torres/Albergo Chileno'.

Take a last look back over Lago Nordenskjöld, before continuing alongside another, smaller **lake**, which you pass on your left (not on your right as marked on the CONAF map). At the far end of this lake you reach a junction, about 3hrs from Refugio Los Cuernos. This makes a good place to stop, with fine views back across the lake. (For those who want to head **direct to Refugio El Chileno** rather than Refugio Las Torres, the trail on the left at the end of the lake provides a 'shortcut' (2hrs from here, ie. 1hr longer than continuing to Refugio Las Torres) – although the trail is less clear than the main route and is not marked on the CONAF map.) ◄

Taking this route is not encouraged because of erosion along the trail.

Continue straight ahead, following the sign to Hostería Las Torres. Follow green trail markers, passing a path on your right then fording a small stream; 30mins beyond the stream you reach a **junction** below a large dark shingle bank. Here you have two choices. The trail on the left leads up to El Chileno, straight ahead leads to Refugio Las Torres. If you plan to visit Mirador Las Torres at dawn, and have booked accommodation accordingly, you need to stay at El Chileno (the old Campamento Torres, for a long time the base for pre-dawn ascents to Mirador Las Torres, is currently closed) – in which case turn left, and allow at least 1hr to reach El Chileno following the route described in Stage 5. If you plan to visit Mirador Las Torres as a day trip but are not trying to reach the towers at dawn, you can continue to the larger Refugio Las Torres, as described below.

Keep straight ahead, crossing the suspension bridge over the Río Ascencio (cross one at a time – the bridge sways quite a bit), then another smaller bridge to reach

a small information kiosk (hours 10am–2pm, 4–8pm) and the huge, sprawling hotel complex of **Hotel Las Torres**, at the far end of a field. The hotel, which seems to grow each year, is owned by the descendants of the original owner of Estancia Cerro Paine, and a large area of this side of the national park is still private land. Turn left along the road in front of Hotel Las Torres to reach **Refugio Las Torres** in a few minutes.

Bridge over the Río Ascencio

> **Refugio Las Torres** has beds in two buildings – Refugio Las Torres Central is the main, newer lodge, and Refugio Las Torres Norte a second, smaller lodge nearby – as well as a large restaurant and bar, and a small shop. The nice campsite, on the W side of the small stream, has plenty of flat grassy sites, as well as its own showers and toilets. There are good views up over Valle Ascencio towards the Torres from the higher ground behind (N of) the campsite.
>
> Just to the NE of Refugio Las Torres is the well-managed **EcoCamp Patagonia**, which has comfortable, dome-like dwellings, good meals, and an impressive commitment to the environment. You'll almost certainly need to have booked to stay here (see Appendix B).

STAGE 5
Refugio Las Torres – El Chileno

Start	Refugio Las Torres
Distance	5.5km
Rating	moderate
Time	1hr 45mins
Maximum altitude	415m
Map	CONAF Parque Nacional Torres del Paine
Accommodation	Refugio Las Torres, Refugio El Chileno (both Fantastico Sur, tel 061 2614 184, www.fantasticosur.com); EcoCamp Patagonia (tel 02 2923 5950 or 0800 051 7095 (toll free from UK), www.ecocamp.travel); Hotel Las Torres (tel 061 2617 450 or 061 2617 451, www.lastorres.com)

Many visitors choose to hike up to Mirador Las Torres and back from Refugio Las Torres, as a day trip. While this carries the alluring prospect of not having to lug a full pack up the valley of the Río Ascencio, it also means that you will not (unless starting very, very early) reach the mirador before dawn – the most dramatic (and photogenic) time to view the towers, when they glow red in the first rays of the sun. You are more likely to find them free of cloud than later in the day, too.) For a dawn visit to the towers, it's better to stay at El Chileno and start from there (unfortunately Campamento Torres, higher up the valley and for a long time the base for pre-dawn ascents to Mirador Las Torres, is currently closed). For those who want to visit Mirador Las Torres as a day trip from Refugio Las Torres, allow around 6hr 30mins to hike up to the mirador and back, 9hr if you plan to visit the upper reaches of the Valle Ascencio as well.

Follow the 4WD track W from **Refugio Las Torres**, passing Hotel Las Torres and retracing your steps over the
suspension bridge to the **junction** below the dark shingle bank, where you turn right. The trail climbs steadily
above the Río Ascencio, with views of steep black scarp
on the far side, then rounds a slightly exposed and tre-
mendously windy bluff, before descending gradually.
Cross the bridge to reach **Refugio El Chileno**, 1hr 45mins
from Refugio Las Torres.

> **El Chileno** is a pleasant little hut with beds as well as a
> sheltered, level area for camping. Campers can use the
> showers and toilets in the hut. If you're staying and plan-
> ning to eat here, you need to book dinner before 6pm.

Rio Ascencio

STAGE 6
El Chileno – Mirador Las Torres
(return)

Start	El Chileno
Distance	7.5km
Rating	moderate
Time	3hrs 30mins (return)
Maximum altitude	1010m
Map	CONAF Parque Nacional Torres del Paine
Accommodation	El Chileno

If you want to see the towers at their most spectacular – and with less chance of cloud than later in the day – set out early, allowing yourself enough time to get up to the lookout well before dawn. Take breakfast, plenty of warm clothes and a torch. It takes at least 2hrs, and more if you're making your way in the dark with a torch. This short route could easily be combined with Stage 7 within one day.

From **El Chileno**, continue along the true left bank of the river before crossing back to the right bank (a path used to continue on the right bank from opposite El Chileno, but was closed recently due to erosion). Ascend through trees, crossing **bridges** over side-streams and passing a split and partly hollow tree, looking like a great twisted piece of rope. Just under 1hr 15mins from El Chileno emerge onto more open slopes, and a **junction**. The trail straight ahead leads to the site of the old Campamento Torres, now closed.

Turn left, and foll ow the trail up alongside the treeline and a small stream. The route climbs up through the enormous boulders of the terminal moraine, with

the occasional cairn and orange marker poles, to reach **Mirador Las Torres** in 45mins from the junction.

A bleak day at Mirador Las Torres

> The view from the **mirador** is magnificent, with the three slender 'towers' rising directly opposite you on the far side of a frigid glacial lake – from left to right these are Torre Sur (the highest, at 2850m), Torre Central (2800m) and Torre Norte (2248m) – and, to the right of these, lies Cerro Nido de Cóndor (2243m). On the left is the broad bulk of Monte Almirante Nieto (2640m).
>
> Keep an eye out for Condors soaring above the crags – and, if you're eating anything, for the small but remarkably bold little mice that scurry out from among the boulders in search of crumbs. The vivid red light on the towers at dawn lasts only a matter of minutes, but it's a wonderful spot where you'll doubtless want to linger rather longer.

Before you head back, you can scramble down over enormous boulders to the shore of the lake. Return to the mirador and descend to **El Chileno** by the same route.

STAGE 7
El Chileno – Campamento Japonés (return)

Start	El Chileno
Distance	7.5km
Rating	moderate
Time	4hrs 45mins (return)
Maximum altitude	710m
Map	CONAF Parque Nacional Torres del Paine
Accommodation	El Chileno

If you've made an early trip up to Mirador Las Torres (Stage 6), you should have enough time to follow the Valle Ascencio up to Campamento Japonés, before either spending a second night at El Chileno or heading back down to Refugio Las Torres.

From **El Chileno**, follow the route described in Stage 6 up to the junction below the trail to Mirador las Torres, then continue straight ahead, passing the site of the old Campamento Torres (closed). Continue up the valley of the Río Ascencio, passing below the boulder fields (there are decent views of the 'towers' from here) that spill down from Mirador Las Torres. The trail leads through forest, crossing two small side-streams before emerging into a large boulder field in 20mins, where the trail becomes less clear. Carry on more or less straight through this, following the odd cairn, before clambering over fallen tree trunks and diving back into the forest, where there are some more small streams to cross and increasingly tortured-looking, shattered trees. ◄

This section of the Río Ascencio is a good place for spotting Torrent Ducks (*Merganetta armata*), which perch out on rocks in the middle of fast-flowing mountains streams such as this.

1hr 10mins from Campamento Torres arrive at **Campamento Japonés**, by a shingle bank with overhanging trees.

Campamento Japonés is, at least officially, only for the use of climbers and mountaineering groups. There is a large, plastic- and tarpaulin-covered shelter here (again, not technically for the use of trekkers), and a rather wonderful little wooden shrine with sculptures of Cranes, made by a group of Korean climbers here in 2007. From the back of the camp a trail heads up into the trees, towards the Valle del Silencio, which is still hidden from view.

Torrent Ducks (female left, male right), in the upper reaches of the Valle Ascensio

Return to **El Chileno** by the same route.

STAGE 8
El Chileno – Refugio Las Torres

Start	El Chileno
Distance	5.5km
Rating	easy
Time	1hr 30mins
Maximum altitude	415m
Map	CONAF Parque Nacional Torres del Paine
Accommodation	El Chileno, Refugio Las Torres

This route back down the Valle Ascencio simply follows Stage 5 in reverse. As it's a short stage you'll have enough time to continue to Campamento Serón without staying an additional night at Refugio Las Torres if you prefer.

Descend from **El Chileno** to **Refugio Las Torres**.

STAGE 9
Refugio Las Torres – Campamento Serón

Start	Refugio Las Torres
Distance	9km
Rating	easy–moderate
Time	4hrs 30mins
Maximum altitude	500m
Map	CONAF Parque Nacional Torres del Paine
Accommodation	Campamento Serón (Fantastico Sur, tel 061 2614 184, www.fantasticosur.com)

This is the first stage of the route to take you off the section shared with the 'W', and onto the north half of the circuit.

Follow the 4WD track N from **Refugio Las Torres**, then after 15mins take a trail which branches off to the left, climbing slightly and passing a sign marked 'Serón'. The path climbs over a shoulder with good views to the S, then enters the forest, at which point you will have a fence on your right.

1hr from Las Torres reach the first of many stream crossings on this stage, then just over 1hr later there is another. Another 15mins brings you to a 'Serón' sign which confirms you're on the right path, before you reach another stream in 30mins. Descend steeply towards grassy flats over which a river meanders lazily, with the **Río Paine** on your right.

Turn right through the fence (where you'll find another 'Serón' sign), before reaching a broad side-stream which you ford (care needed after heavy rain). Continue across the flats, crossing various small channels, before veering left and crossing a bridge over a small stream. This is followed by a succession of small bridges (one of them a single log), before the path continues close to the bank of the Río Paine to arrive at **Campamento Serón**, 4hrs 30mins from Refugio Las Torres.

Campamento Serón lies at the edge of wide, daisy-covered flats, where there is a good chance of seeing Black-faced Ibis grazing in the meadows, while Ruffous-collared Sparrows hop among the tent sites. There is a small warden's hut, a tap with drinking water and a shower.

STAGE 10
Campamento Serón – Refugio Dickson

Start	Campamento Serón
Distance	18.5km
Rating	moderate
Time	6hrs 15mins
Maximum altitude	470m
Map	CONAF Parque Nacional Torres del Paine
Accommodation	Campamento Serón (Fantastico Sur, tel 061 2614 184, www.fantasticosur.com); Refugio Dickson (Vertice, tel 061 2412 742 or 061 2415 693, www.verticepatagonia.com). Camp Coiron (marked on some maps but not on the CONAF one), just SW of Lago Paine, is no longer in use; in fact there is little sign of a possible campsite in this area – and it is not recognised by CONAF as a permissible place to camp.

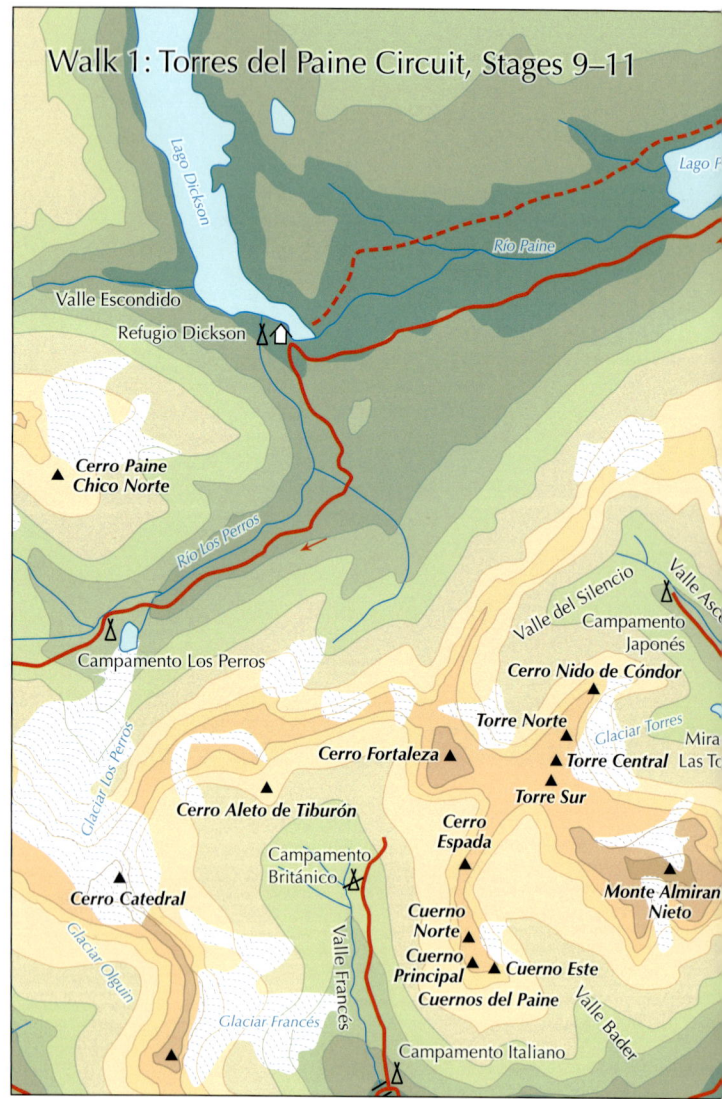

Walk 1: Torres del Paine Circuit, Stages 9–11

Lago Dickson

Lago P

Río Paine

Valle Escondido

Refugio Dickson

▲ *Cerro Paine Chico Norte*

Río Los Perros

Campamento Los Perros

Valle del Silencio

Valle Asc

Campamento Japonés

Cerro Nido de Cóndor

Glaciar Los Perros

Torre Norte ▲

Glaciar Torres

Mira

Cerro Fortaleza ▲

▲ *Torre Central* Las To

Torre Sur

▲ *Cerro Aleto de Tiburón*

Cerro Espada

Glaciar Los Perros

Cerro Catedral ▲

Campamento Británico

▲ *Monte Almiran Nieto*

Cuerno Norte ▲

Glaciar Olguin

Valle Francés

Cuerno Principal ▲ *Cuerno Este*

Cuernos del Paine

Valle Bader

Glaciar Francés

Campamento Italiano

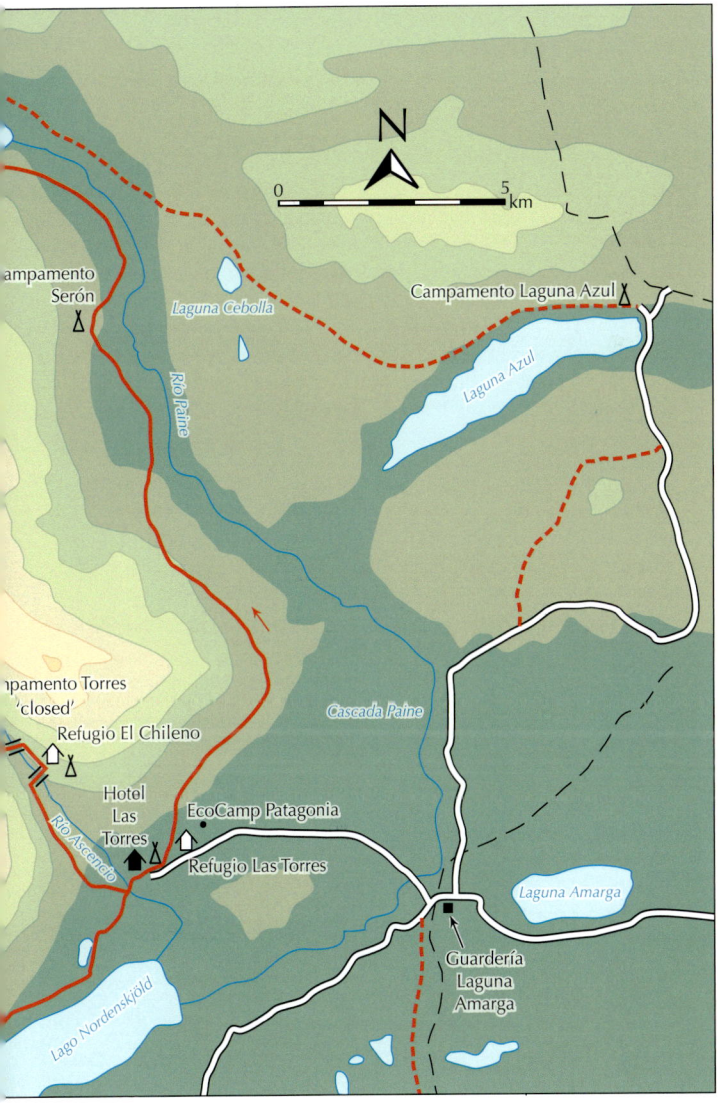

A fairly long stage, crossing a remarkably blustery saddle, and with some lovely sections alongside the Río Paine.

Follow the trail NE from **Campamento Serón**, heading for the river then continuing left along the true right bank of the Río Paine. Cross a side-stream, but choose a point slightly further upstream (left) if the water is high. The trail then heads over headlands and around bluffs and an inlet before climbing steeply over a spur. After the switchbacks the trail levels off slightly, passing through prominent clumps of Mata Barrosa (*Mulinum spinosum*), before reaching a shoulder, exposed to the full force of the wind (it was hard to stand up when I was last here), about 90mins from Serón.

There are lovely views of the mountains ahead, if you get the chance to look at them before descending to the relative shelter of the path ahead. The lake below on the right is **Lago Paine**. After crossing another shoulder the trail descends, with a waterfall on the left, and crosses a small stream where water flasks can be refilled. Continue, then descend steeply, crossing small streams and passing another waterfall and heading through some trees.

Mata Barrosa (Mulinum spinosum)

Just over 3hrs from Serón you reach a somewhat larger stream. There is a precarious, single-log 'bridge' a short distance along, which you may choose to cross – although a slip here will leave you very wet indeed. If the water is not too high, you may be able to ford the stream near here; otherwise, continue a bit further and ford the stream where it is braided and shallower – although if you cross here you will have to wade through a broad, marshy area with stagnant pools on the other side before reaching the path again. Continue, crossing more small streams then following sections of boardwalk (this was unfinished in 2009, leaving a final boggy area to wade through). Carry on across flats, then up onto a shoulder from where Refugio Dickson finally comes into view, nested on the far side of the grassy flats below. Descend steeply, then cross the pleasant grassy flats to reach **Refugio Dickson** in 15mins.

On the trail above Lago Paine, between Campamento Serón and Refugio Dickson

Cerro Paine Chico Norte from Refugio Dickson

Refugio Dickson is one of the most pleasant huts on the Circuit – beautifully situated, with friendly staff, and less crowded than those on the 'W' (the mosquitoes, however, are almost unbelievably ferocious, particularly if you arrive in January/February). There are toilets, sinks and showers (at least one of them hot) outside for the use of campers. In the hut breakfast is served 7.30–9.30am ($5900), lunch 12am–2pm ($7000) and dinner 7.30–9pm ($10,500). As usual, reserve a few hours ahead (dinner) or the previous evening (breakfast). Packed lunches are also available.

There are fine views north across Lago Dickson to Glaciar Dickson and surrounding peaks – just beyond which is the border with Argentina, where arms of the South Patagonian Ice Field spill down towards Lago Argentino, including the Perito Moreno glacier – and southwest to Cerro Paine Chico Norte.

STAGE 11
Refugio Dickson – Campamento Los Perros

Start	Refugio Dickson
Distance	9km
Rating	moderate
Time	4hrs 30mins
Maximum altitude	665m
Map	CONAF Parque Nacional Torres del Paine
Accommodation	Refugio Dickson, Campamento Los Perros (both Vertice, tel 061 2412 742 or 061 2415 693, www.verticepatagonia.com)

This stage offers fantastic views of Glaciar Dickson and Glaciar Los Perros as you ascend gradually into the more remote northern section of the Circuit.

From **Refugio Dickson** head roughly S, following the 'Perros' sign. The trail ascends gradually, through forest and over the occasional log bridge, with intermittent views back to the mountains N of Lago Dickson. After about 1hr 15mins pass an open, level area on the left of the trail, and reach a slightly raised area on the right, with clear views ahead and back. Carry on, crossing a well-made wooden bridge, and some 25mins later pass a huge waterfall on your right.

The trail continues, crossing the occasional stream before reaching a bridge over a deep river gorge, with views of glaciers on the left. Continue with the river now on your left, and with moraines and glaciers ahead.

Cross a bridge back onto the true right bank of the **Río Los Perros** and rocky open moraine, with scattered young beech, then ascend onto the moraine, with views over the lake below to the enormous tumbling mass of Glaciar Los Perros, bristling with ice towers. Veer to

Glaciar Los Perros, from the trail above Refugio Dickson

your right, descending slightly and weaving through boulder fields, then around another moraine to arrive at **Campamento Los Perros**, sheltered in the trees close to the bank of the river.

At **Campamento Los Perros** there is a small warden's office and a large plastic- and tarpaulin-covered communal mess tent, as well as toilets, cold showers and water tap; camping is $3500 per person. The bouldery flats by the river are relatively mosquito free. The name 'Los Perros' apparently commemorates two dogs ('dog' is *perro* in Spanish), which were drowned in the river near here.

Once you've pitched your tent, it's worth heading back around – or better, over – the moraine behind the campsite to the lake below Glaciar Los Perros. It's a lovely quiet spot, with slowly melting icebergs drifting along the shore.

Check the forecast for tomorrow, as the Circuit crosses Paso John Gardner, which can be extremely windy. The CONAF officers at Los Perros will have up-to-date weather forecasts, and are under instructions to discourage (or even prevent) trekkers from trying to cross the pass in poor weather and high winds. Be prepared, in extreme cases, to stay at Los Perros an extra day.

STAGE 12

Campamento Los Perros – Campamento Paso

Start	Campamento Los Perros
Distance	12km
Rating	difficult
Time	5hrs 30mins
Maximum altitude	1180m
Map	CONAF Parque Nacional Torres del Paine
Accommodation	Campamento Los Perros (Vertice, tel 061 2412 742 or 061 2415 693, www.verticepatagonia.com); Campamento Paso

The route over Paso John Gardner, while not technically difficult, is exposed to the full force of the wind, which fairly blasts straight into the pass from the Southern Patagonian Ice Field. Though some route descriptions give the timing for this stage as only 4hrs 30mins, you are advised to allow longer.

Follow the increasingly steep and muddy trail from **Campamento Los Perros**, crossing a succession of side-streams then finally emerging above the tree line, 1hr from last night's campsite. Continue over boulders and

On the trail to Paso John Gardner

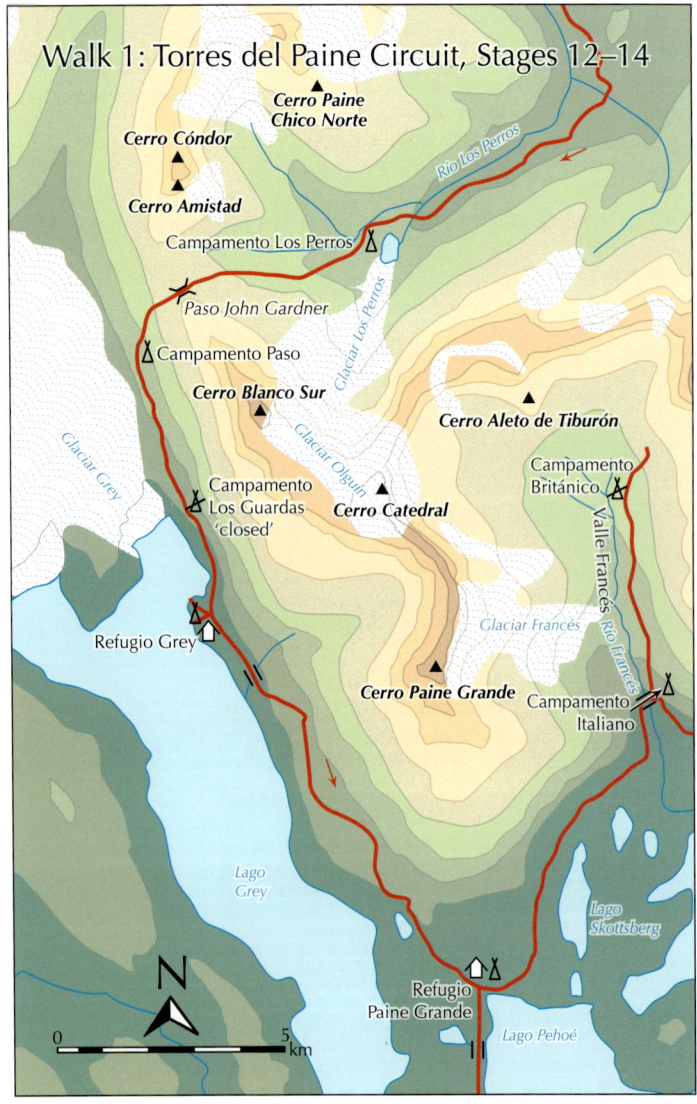

Walk 1: Torres del Paine Circuit, Stages 12–14

*Cerro Paine
Chico Norte*

Cerro Cóndor

Cerro Amistad

Campamento Los Perros

Río Los Perros

Paso John Gardner

Glaciar Los Perros

Campamento Paso

Cerro Blanco Sur

Cerro Aleto de Tiburón

Glaciar Olguín

Campamento
Británico

Glaciar Grey

Campamento
Los Guardas
'closed'

Cerro Catedral

Valle Francés

Río Francés

Glaciar Francés

Refugio Grey

Cerro Paine Grande

Campamento
Italiano

Lago
Grey

Lago
Skottsberg

N

0   5
km

Refugio
Paine Grande

Lago Pehoé

rock, before (rather annoyingly) being forced to drop back down into the trees.

The trail heads up again over boulders, descending a couple more times to the tree line before continuing alongside a narrow gorge on your right. The pass is clearly visible ahead now, together with an enormous blue glacier to the right below Cerro Amistad and Cerro Cóndor. Continue along a faint trail, with braided streams on your right, crossing channels and heading across boulders and areas of tundra. Ascend left to reach **Paso John Gardner** (1180m), 3hrs from Campamento Los Perros.

The views from the pass are jaw-dropping. Ahead and below sprawls the enormous expanse of fractured blue ice that is Glaciar Grey, some 6km wide at this point yet nevertheless constituting a mere finger of ice at the edge the vast Campo de Hielo Sur. Behind you the valley drops down to trees and the Río Los Perros, below a row of jagged peaks on the right – Cerro Blanco Sur and its satellites – behind which the upper reaches of Glaciar Los Perros are hidden from view.

Probably equally breathtaking will be the wind, which howls over the pass from the Southern Patagonian Ice Field to the W. There's a small, low stone enclosure which provides a modicum of shelter, but if the wind's even moderately up – gusts of up to 100km/h and more are not uncommon – you'll probably want to move on from this magnificent spot fairly swiftly.

If visibility is poor, make sure you have a clear idea of the route ahead before descending – although it is perfectly straightforward in clear weather, you could easily become lost on this largely featureless slope in poor visibility. The trail descends, veering first right and then left over rocky slopes, still exposed to the wind, following occasional orange-topped marker poles.

Just over 30mins below the pass, the trail enters low trees, becoming steps which descend steeply with the aid of a handrail. Pass a couple of small, level spots just large enough for a tent on your right and left, with occasional views of Glaciar Grey through the trees. Follow a section of wooden boardwalk, then ascend slightly, crossing first

Descending from Paso John Gardner above Glaciar Grey

one then another bridge over side-streams, the second of which is larger and has clear views out over Glaciar Grey.

Cross another small side-stream, passing a couple of good viewpoints on the right. ◄ Then ascend slightly again to reach **Campamento Paso**, 2hrs 15mins from the pass.

Head down to the rocky slopes on your right, just above the glacier, for excellent views.

Campamento Paso has free, numbered tent sites, a toilet and a small *guardería*; water can be collected from the stream. The elevated terrace just before the camp has good views out over the glacier – but for the best views in this area, head to the viewpoint 10mins back along the trail.

STAGE 13

Campamento Paso – Refugio Grey

Start	Campamento Paso
Distance	10km
Rating	moderate–difficult
Time	3hrs 30mins
Maximum altitude	570m
Map	CONAF Parque Nacional Torres del Paine
Accommodation	Campamento Paso; Refugio Grey (Vertice, tel 061 2412 742 or 061 2415 693, www.verticepatagonia.com)

A section of this stage involves crossing a deep, heavily eroded gully and can take longer than expected (allow 2hrs 20mins to the old Los Guardas campsite).

Cross the bridge over the steam beyond **Campamento Paso**, gaining a good viewpoint before descending and crossing side-streams, then ascending again slightly.

The trail above Glaciar Grey

Crossing a steep gully above Glaciar Grey

Continue over open slopes with shattered, weathered tree trunks. Ascend and descend again, crossing the occasional side-stream, to reach the first gully, 45mins from last night's campsite. The sides of this and the following gullies are heavily eroded, with plenty of loose rock. Descend into the gully, find a suitable place to ford or jump the fast-flowing river channels, then ascend the steel ladder on the other side.

After a short distance, ascend a short wooden ladder then steep steps. The trail follows another boardwalk, enters trees and then descends, crossing small side-streams. 1hr from the first gully cross another steep ravine on a bridge (formerly you had descend into the gully on a steel ladder), and continue to reach the site of the old Campamento Los Guardas (closed) in about 20mins, or 2hrs 20mins from Campamento Paso.

While you can't camp at **Los Gaurdas**, it's worth stopping to make a short detour here to an excellent viewpoint – just follow the 'mirador' sign on the right to reach a mostly open slope just above the edge of Glaciar Grey in 2mins – a perfect spot for lunch.

Carry on from **Los Guardas**, reaching another gully in 20mins, and this time descend with the aid of a rope (which was loose, on my last visit). Beyond the gully another boardwalk is reached, followed by a rocky terrace with views out over the snout of Glaciar Grey and a small bay at the head of Lago Grey, backed by moraine and scattered with icebergs. A faint path on the right descends to a grassy area surrounded by Calafate and Firebushes – another good spot for a rest. Continue along the main trail, crossing an open area with scattered trees on a broad clear path, and passing the rather unhelpful sign pointing back in the direction you have just come: 'Refugio Dickson 14hrs'. Continue past this then turn right, descending to the beach and **Refugio Grey**.

Refugio Grey is a lovely spot, situated on a small bay on Lago Grey, where diminutive icebergs float in to melt under the warm sun. It's also very busy, being only a 3hr 30min hike from Refugio Paine Grande and the catamaran to Pudeto – so pick a decent site sooner rather than later if you're camping. Camping around the bay is $3500 per person, or $22,000 full board; beds in the hut go for $34,000 full board. Dinner is served 7–8pm ($10,500; order before 5.30pm); breakfast 7.30–9am ($5900; order by 10pm the night before); order lunch by 11.30am, and packed lunches by 10pm the night before. At the hut you can also arrange 'ice trekking' on the lower reaches of the glacier.

While you're here, it's well worth heading back along the main trail a short distance, then branching off to the left on a trail which brings you to a rocky promontory overlooking the snout of Glaciar Grey and La Isla, the small island which this mountainous flow of ice slowly and steadily flows into – this is about as close as you can get without heading out on a boat trip. Allow 1hr return.

STAGE 14
Refugio Grey – Refugio Paine Grande

Start	Refugio Grey
Distance	11km
Rating	easy–moderate
Time	4hrs 15mins
Maximum altitude	375m
Map	CONAF Parque Nacional Torres del Paine
Accommodation	Refugio Grey, Refugio Paine Grande (both Vertice, tel 061 2412 742 or 061 2415 693, www.verticepatagonia.com)

The final stage of the Circuit takes you high above Lago Grey and past lonely windswept tarns before descending through lush Firebushes to Refugio Paine Grande.

Head back along the broad, clear trail from **Refugio Grey**, passing the trails to the promontory overlooking the snout of the glacier and to Campamento Paso on the left. The trail is fairly level, following sections of boardwalk and passing a small canyon on the right, followed by a good viewpoint.

Continue, passing a large waterfall on the left and then the canyon below it with rapids, also on the left. Descend, with views of the canyon on the left and a lake on the right, and cross a **bridge** over the canyon (Puente Olguin). Follow more boardwalks, then double back (left) and ascend through trees before veering right again. Continue over slightly exposed rocky sections, crossing three small side-streams, then ascend to another good viewpoint, about 2hrs 20mins from Refugio Grey.

Not far to go now – something you may find either comforting or rather disappointing. Pass small lakes on your right (keep an eye out for wildfowl here), then head

over open tops with more shattered tree trunks, with fine views SW to the Pingo glacier and a line of peaks to the SSE.

Peaks above the eastern side of Glaciar Grey

The trail continues, ascending then veering left and crossing more side-streams, with flats on the right and a **lake** coming into view ahead. Laguna Los Patos ('duck lake'), which you pass on your right, is quite large and very idyllic, with views of mountains beyond, and has a nice spot to rest at the far end – although it does tend to be fairly windy here. Despite its name you might find less wildfowl here than on the smaller, more sheltered lakes passed earlier on this stage.

Descend into a valley, meandering through Firebushes with the huge spiky ramparts of Cerro Paine Grande on your left, and the almost other-worldly vivid turquoise of Lago Pehoé ahead, before striding back into **Refugio Paine Grande** – the end of the Torres del Paine Circuit. (See Stage 1 for information on the refuge.)

Catamaran at Refugio Paine Grande on Lago Pehoé

If you've completed the entire Circuit (or the 'Q', as it has been described here), then congratulations are in order, and you're doubtless in for a well-earned rest. From here you can take the catamaran across Lago Pehoé to Pudeto in the morning and visit **Salto Grande** (see Walk 3), before catching the bus back to Puerto Natales (or Lago Toro, for the Río Pingo trek, Walk 7). If you didn't walk in from the CONAF Administración at Lago Toro at the beginning of your trek, it's well worth taking one more day to head down to **Lago Toro** (follow Stage 1 in reverse).

The catamaran to Pudeto leaves from the small jetty by Refugio Paine Grande at 10am, 12.30am and 6.30pm. Buy tickets (cash only) in advance if possible, or queue early to make sure you get a place.

WALK 2

Torres del Paine half-circuit (the 'W')

Start/Finish	Refugio Las Torres/Refugio Paine Grande
Distance	70.5km
Duration	5 days
Maps	See sketch maps and the CONAF map given free when paying your entrance fee to the national park.
Transport	To get to the start of the trek, either take the bus from Puerto Natales to Laguna Amarga, followed by the shuttle to Refugio Las Torres (or you can walk this section in 1hr – see the beginning of Walk 1), or, if starting from Refugio Paine Grande, stay on the bus from Puerto Natales as far as Pudeto, then take the catamaran across Lago Pehoé to Refugio Paine Grande. See 'Transport to and around the park' in the Introduction for bus and catamaran times.
Accommodation	There are now huts and camping for all stages – if you don't want to camp, you can stay in one of the geodomes at Campamento/Domos Francés on Stages 2/3 or cut Stage 2 short at Refugio Los Cuernos. (You may then need to reduce the length of the walk in the Valle Francés, Stage 3.) Further accommodation options are EcoCamp Patagonia and Hotel Las Torres (Stage 1). See Appendix B for a full list of huts and campsites.

The 'W' follows the southern section of the Circuit beween Refugio Paine Grande and Refugio Las Torres, with visits to Refugio Grey, the Valle Francés and the Valle Ascencio, thus taking in many – but not all – of the longer route's highlights. What the 'W' misses are the more open, remote sections of the national park further north and the crossing of Paso John Gardner. But it can be walked in four to five days, and (at least partly for this reason) is the more popular of the two treks, and far busier than the northern section of the Circuit.

Even though the 'W' can be walked from either end, you would be advised to base this choice on the weather

Spectacular peaks above Glaciar Grey

conditions – if fine, start from the east and make the most of the clear weather to head up the Valle Ascencio and see the spectacular 'towers'; if not, start from the west and hope the weather clears up by the time you get there. The route is described here from east to west.

If you want to walk the other way (ie. starting from Refugio Paine Grande), to reach the start point take the bus from Puerto Natales as far as Pudeto, then take the catamaran across Lago Pehoé to Refugio Paine Grande. Head straight up to Refugio Grey for the first night (if you're on an early catamaran), or stop at Refugio Paine Grande and visit Refugio Grey as a day trip (if you arrive on a later catamaran). Then, from Refugio Paine Grande simply follow the route description in Walk 1, Stages 2–8 in reverse.

Note that Refugio Paine Grande is marked as Refugio Pehoé on some maps.

STAGE 1

Refugio Las Torres – Mirador Las Torres (return)

Start	Refugio Las Torres
Distance	11.5km
Rating	moderate
Time	3hrs
Maximum altitude	1010m
Map	CONAF Parque Nacional Torres del Paine
Accommodation	Refugio Las Torres, Refugio El Chileno (both Fantastico Sur, tel 061 2614 184, www.fantasticosur.com); EcoCamp Patagonia (tel 02 2923 5950 or 0800 051 7095 (toll free from UK), www.ecocamp.travel); Hotel Las Torres (tel 061 2617 450 or 061 2617 451, www.lastorres.com)

The following excursion visits the Valle Ascencio and Mirador Las Torres – a viewpoint over the spectacular 'towers' – as a day trip from Refugio Las Torres. However, to see the famous towers at their most picturesque, at sunrise, you should stay at El Chileno, get up before dawn and walk up from there to the mirador.

Refugio Las Torres has beds in two buildings – Torres Central is the main, newer lodge, and Torres Norte is a second, smaller lodge nearby – as well as a large restaurant and bar, and a small shop. There is a good campsite, on the W side of the small stream, with plenty of flat grassy sites, as well as its own showers and toilets. There are good views up over Valle Ascencio towards the 'towers' from the higher ground behind (N of) the campsite. Just to the NE of Refugio Las Torres is EcoCamp Patagonia, with comfortable,

109

The Torres del Paine

dome-like dwellings (you will almost certainly need to have booked in advance to stay here).

From **Refugio Las Torres**, follow the road past **Hotel Las Torres**, veer right across a field and cross a suspension bridge over the Río Ascencio. Turn right at the junction below the dark shingle bank, climbing steadily above the Río Ascencio. After rounding a slightly exposed and very windy bluff, the trail descends to a bridge over the river to reach **Refugio El Chileno**, 1hr 45mins from Refugio Las Torres.

> **El Chileno** has beds in the hut as well as a sheltered, level area for camping; campers can use the showers and toilets in the hut. Book dinner before 6pm.

Continue along the true left bank of the river before crossing a bridge back to the right bank and ascending through forest to reach a junction just above the old **Campamento Torres** (closed), just under 1hr 15mins from El Chileno. Turn left up by the tree line, then carry on over enormous boulders to reach **Mirador Las Torres** in 45mins, with spectacular views of the three 'towers'. Descend to **Refugio Las Torres** by the same route.

STAGE 2

Refugio Las Torres – Campamento Italiano

Start	Refugio Las Torres
Distance	16.5km
Rating	easy–moderate
Time	6hrs 15mins
Maximum altitude	235m
Map	CONAF Parque Nacional Torres del Paine
Accommodation	Refugio Las Torres, Refugio Los Cuernos (both Fantastico Sur, tel 061 2614 184, www.fantasticosur.com); Campamento Italiano, Camp Francés

A fairly long stage, with beautiful views across Lago Nordenskjold. For those who want a shorter day (or who don't wish to camp) it's possible to stay the night at Refugio Los Cuernos before visiting the lower reaches of the Valle Francés as a (longish) day trip or simply continuing to Refugio Paine Grande.

From **Refugio Las Torres**, walk past **Hotel Las Torres** again and cross the suspension bridge over the Río Ascencio, then turn left at the junction with the trail up to Mirador Las Torres, following the sign marked 'Albergo Los Cuernos'. Ford a small stream, then veer right (not straight ahead) to arrive at a junction at the head of a lake, 1hr from Refugio Las Torres.

The trail on the right provides an unofficial 'short-cut' to Refugio El Chileno. Keep straight ahead, on the left side of the lake (not right as marked on the CONAF map), before descending slightly with views over Lago Nordenskjöld. Cross a succession of side-streams by a variety of low wooden bridges and fords (care needed after heavy rain), then ascend over a shoulder before descending to **Refugio Los Cuernos**, 4hrs from Refugion Las Torres.

Refugio Los Cuernos (also known as Albergo Los Cuernos) has beds in the hut as well as several small cabins, and camping among the bushes nearby. It serves breakfast, lunch and dinner.

For those who don't wish to walk the entirety of today's stage to Campamento Italiano, it would be possible to break the route by staying overnight at Refugio Los Cuernos. From here it is possible to visit the lower reaches of the Valle Francés as a (longish) day trip, or simply to continue to Refugio Paine Grande.

Continue past Refugio Los Cuernos, following pebble beaches alongside the shore of Lago Nordenskjöld then ascending over a shoulder. Cross more streams and follow sections of wooden boardwalk, veering gradually right, to reach **Campamento/Domos Francés**.

Campamento/Domos Francés is a serviced campsite with three large geodomes, and serves breakfast and dinner.

Continue to arrive at **Campamento Italiano** in the Valle Francés, 2hrs 15mins from Refugio Los Cuernos.

Campamento Italiano lies scattered along the bank of the Río Francés, sheltered among the trees. The *guardería* and larger camping area are slightly further upstream; the quieter campsites tend to be those slightly downstream, but so is the toilet. Camping here is free. There are stupendous views of the massive E face of Cerro Paine Grande from the open, boulder-strewn area by the river.

STAGE 3
Campamento Italiano – Valle Francés (return)

Start	Campamento Italiano
Distance	13km
Rating	moderate
Time	5hrs (return)
Maximum altitude	835m
Map	CONAF Parque Nacional Torres del Paine
Accommodation	Campamento Italiano; Campamento Británico

This excursion into the spectacular and remote-feeling Valle Francés could easily be combined with the walk to Refugio Paine Grande (the first half of Stage 4) on the same day. Alternatively, for those who wish to linger in the area, there's a further campsite (less busy than Campamento Italiano) up towards the head of the Valle Francés, Campamento Británico.

Head N from **Campamento Italiano**, following the true left bank of the Río Francés and climbing gradually. As you gain height there are amazing views of the huge E face of Cerro Paine Grande, with the Glaciar Francés sprawling below.

Glacier above the massive east face of Cerro Paine Grande, from the Valle Francés

Cross a side-stream after 30mins, just below a waterfall, then pass a large stream to reach a clearing with wind-blasted tree stumps and wonderful views back over the intense turquoise of Lago Nordenskjöld. Continue, crossing minor streams to reach a large rocky clearing (good views of Cerro Fortaleza on the right, as well as the 'back' of the Cuernos), before arriving at **Campamento Británico**, hidden in the trees on the other side of the river, 2hrs 30mins from Campamento Italiano.

Campamento Británico is fairly basic, but quieter than Camapamento Italiano and feels wonderfully remote; camping here is free. It was from this base that a British team climbed Cerro Fortaleza in 1968.

The trail climbs gradually from Campamento Británico, with the huge panorama of peaks at the head of Valle Francés opening up before you, to reach the mirador (viewpoint) in 20mins. This is little more than a small rock outcrop, and the views from it not that much better than those 5mins below it; but it's a wonderful spot nonetheless, with one of the finest views in the national park. The prominent, fin-like peak is Cerro Aleto de Tiburón ('shark's fin').

Descend to **Campamento Italiano** by the same route.

STAGE 4
Campamento Italiano – Refugio Grey

Start	Campamento Italiano
Distance	18.5km
Rating	easy–moderate
Time	6hrs 45mins
Maximum altitude	375m
Map	CONAF Parque Nacional Torres del Paine
Accommodation	Campamento Italiano; Refugio Paine Grande, Refugio Grey (both Vertice, tel 061 2412 742 or 061 2415 693, www.verticepatagonia.com)

Another easy although slightly longer stage, to Refugio Paine Grande then north above Lago Grey to Refugio Grey.

From **Campamento Italiano**, cross the bridge over the Río Francés one at a time – do not attempt to ford the river – then a smaller bridge. Continue, following sections of wooden boardwalk. The trail climbs slightly, with stunning views back towards the Cuernos and the line of peaks above the Valle Francés – Cerro Fortaleza, Cerro Espada and Cuerno Este.

Cross a windy shoulder then descend to **Refugio Paine Grande**, 2hrs 30mins from Campamento Italiano. (See Stage 5, below, for details of Refugio Paine Grande.)

Follow the trail up behind the lodge, through a valley filled with *Notro* (Firebush), and passing the attractive Lago Los Patos ('duck lake') on your left. Continue over open tops with shattered tree trunks, passing more small lakes on your left (look out for wildfowl), with good views W over Lago Grey.

The snout of Glaciar Grey

There are excellent views of the snout of Glaciar Grey from a small promontory a little way on from the junction – allow 1hr return; see Walk 1, Stage 13.

Descend through trees, continue on boardwalks and cross a bridge (Puente Oguin) over a small canyon. Ascend slightly, passing a large waterfall on your right and then a small canyon on your left, to arrive at a junction. ◀ Turn left and descend to **Refugio Grey**, 4hrs 15mins from Refugio Paine Grande.

Refugio Grey sits on the edge of a small bay on Lago Grey, where fragments of icebergs float up against the sandy beach. It tends to get fairly busy, being only a 3hr 30min hike from Refugio Paine Grande and the catamaran to Pudeto – so pick a decent site sooner rather than later if you're camping. Camping down around the bay is $3500 per person, or $22,000 full board; beds in the hut go for $34,000 full board. Dinner is served 7–8pm ($10,500; order before 5.30pm) and breakfast 7.30–9am ($5900; order by 10pm the night before). Order lunch by 11.30am, and packed lunches by 10pm the night before. At the refuge you can also arrange 'ice trekking' on the lower reaches of the glacier.

STAGE 5
Refugio Grey – Refugio Paine Grande

Start	Refugio Grey
Distance	11km
Rating	easy–moderate
Time	4hrs 15mins
Maximum altitude	375m
Map	CONAF Parque Nacional Torres del Paine
Accommodation	Refugio Paine Grande, Refugio Grey (both Vertice, tel 061 2412 742 or 061 2415 693, www.verticepatagonia.com)

This route simply retraces a large part of Stage 4.

Return to **Refugio Paine Grande** by the same route.

Cloud formations above Cuernos del Paine, from Refugio Paine Grande

Refugio Paine Grande is a spacious lodge at the north end of Lago Pehoé. The large restaurant has good meals, and there is a small (but noisy) bar upstairs. Campsites are scattered behind and E of the lodge (where it tends to be quieter) – try to choose a site in the lee of the thick bushes, as the wind from the N can be quite strong. The camping office is around the back of the lodge, by the small (although not surprisingly, quite expensive) minimarket. Wooden boardwalks lead from behind the lodge to toilets and showers, and there's also a pleasant little wooden *quincho* – a small pavilion that functions as a communal dining area. The restaurant serves dinner 7–8pm, breakfast 7.30–9am, and lunch 12am–2pm.

The **ferry to Pudeto** (the start point of a short route to Salto Grande and Mirador Los Cuernos; see Walk 3) leaves from the small jetty by Refugio Paine Grande at 10am, 12.30am and 6.30pm. Buy tickets (cash only) in advance if possible, or queue early to make sure you get a place. Alternatively, you could take an extra day to walk out to the CONAF Administración on Lago Toro (5hrs 45mins. See Walk 1, Stage 1 (in reverse).

WALK 3
Salto Grande and Mirador Los Cuernos

Start/Finish	bus/catamaran departure point, Pudeto
Distance	7km
Rating	easy
Time	2hrs 30mins (return)
Maximum altitude	135m
Map	CONAF Parque Nacional Torres del Paine
Transport	Pudeto is on the bus route between Puerto Nalates and the CONAF Administración office on Lago Toro, and is the departure point for catamarans across Lago Pehoé to Refugio Paine Grande.
Accommodation	Aim to complete this route on the way to, or from, Refugio Paine Grande or the CONAF Administración office on Lago Toro. From Refugio Paine Grande (Vertice, tel 061 2412 742 or 061 2415 693, www.verticepatagonia.com), take the morning catamaran over to Pudeto, and return on the 6pm service. Alternatively, the nearest accommodation is Hostería Pehoé (www.hosteriapehoe.cl) or Camping Pehoé (tel 02 196 0377, main office in Punta Arenas tel 061 2249 581, www.campingpehoe.com).

A short walk with spectacular views of the roaring falls of Salto Grande and out across Lago Nordenskjöld to the Cuernos – one of the most iconic vistas in the national park.

Follow the road W from the bus/ferry departure point at **Pudeto** for about 5mins, passing an unsealed road on your right, then turning right into a small parking area. Beyond this you'll find the roaring mass of water which is **Salto Grande** (you'll hear the falls before you see them). ◄ Salto Grande ('large falls') flows between Lago Nordenskjöld and Lago Pehoé;

You can follow a trail down to a rocky, spray-drenched promontory just above the falls.

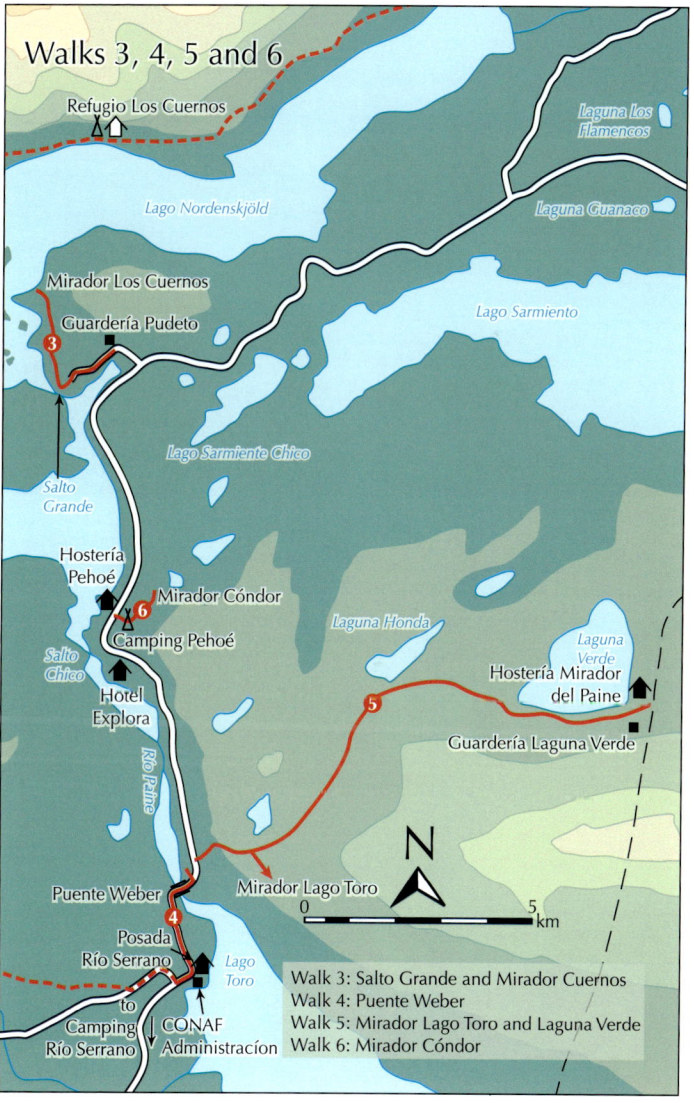

Walks 3, 4, 5 and 6

Refugio Los Cuernos

Laguna Los Flamencos

Lago Nordenskjöld

Laguna Guanaco

Mirador Los Cuernos

Guardería Pudeto

Lago Sarmiento

3

Lago Sarmiente Chico

Salto Grande

Hostería Pehoé

Mirador Cóndor

Laguna Honda

Laguna Verde

6

Camping Pehoé

Hostería Mirador del Paine

5

Guardería Laguna Verde

Hotel Explora

Salto Chico

Río Paine

Mirador Lago Toro

N

0   5 km

Puente Weber

4

Posada Río Serrano

Lago Toro

Walk 3: Salto Grande and Mirador Cuernos
Walk 4: Puente Weber
Walk 5: Mirador Lago Toro and Laguna Verde
Walk 6: Mirador Cóndor

to Camping Río Serrano

CONAF Administracíon

Salto Grande

the latter then drains south into the Río Paine over another set of falls, Salto Chico ('small falls'), and on into Lago Toro.

Follow the marked tail on the right, meandering through scrub and marshland to reach **Mirador Los Cuernos** in 1hr. From here, weather permitting, you'll have magnificent views across Lago Nordenskjöld to the dramatic Cuernos or 'horns'. Return by the same route.

WALK 4
Puente Weber

Start/Finish	CONAF Administración
Distance	5.5km
Rating	easy
Time	1hr 20mins (return)
Maximum altitude	80m
Map	CONAF Parque Nacional Torres del Paine
Transport	The bus from Puerto Natales picks up and drops off outside the CONAF Administración office by Lago Toro.
Accommodation	If, after completing this route, you are starting on the Circuit, you can head from the CONAF Administración office for Refugio Paine Grande (5hrs 45mins; Vertice, tel 061 2412 742 or 061 2415 693, www.verticepatagonia.com); see Walk 1, Stage 1. Closer to the CONAF office is Posada Río Serrano (tel 061 2613 531). Camping Río Serrano (www.horseridingpatagonia.com), about 6km S of the CONAF office, will pick guests up.

A very short, easy walk to the Puente Weber (Weber Bridge) on the Río Paine, with excellent views. For those arriving early at the CONAF office on Lago Grey for the start of Walk 1, this can easily be fitted in first.

From the **CONAF Administración office** on Lago Toro hike back (N) along the road to cross the old wooden **Puente Weber** (Weber Bridge), which spans the Río Paine here. Avoid crossing the bridge when there's traffic.

Head up the small rise on the other side of the river for superlative views N to the Cuernos across the Río Paine, and S over undulating Mata Barrosa (*Mulinum*

View of the Paine massif across the Río Paine, from between Puente Weber and the trail to Mirador Lago Toro

spinosum) and other vivid greenery towards Lago Toro. Return to the **CONAF office** by the same route.

For those with still more time on their hands, the trail to **Mirador Lago Toro and Laguna Verde** (Walk 5) starts a short distance along the road from Puente Weber, on the right.

WALK 5

Mirador Lago Toro and Laguna Verde

Start/Finish	Road N of Puente Weber (see Walk 4)
Distance	4.5km (return to Mirador Lago Toro), or 26.5km (return to Laguna Verde)
Rating	easy–moderate
Time	1hr 30mins (return to Mirador Lago Toro), or 9hrs 30mins (return to Laguna Verde)
Maximum altitude	456m
Map	CONAF Parque Nacional Torres del Paine (**Note** Mirador Lago Toro is marked as Mirador Toro on some maps.)
Transport	Buses between Puerto Natales and the CONAF Administración office pass the beginning of this walk. There's no official stop here, but ask to be let off the bus at the trail to Laguna Verde or at Puente Weber. Buses won't pick up here, so for onward travel walk instead down (S) to the CONAF Administración office on Lago Toro.
Accommodation	Early arrival at the CONAF Administración office on Lago Toro will give you enough time to complete this and Walk 4 to the Puente Weber. On the road (and bus route) further N there's Camping Pehoé (tel 02 196 0377; main office in Punta Arenas tel 061 2249 581; www.campingpehoe.com). Otherwise, there's nearby Posada Río Serrano (tel 061 2613 531). If you're continuing to Laguna Verde, there's Hostería Mirador del Paine (tel 061 2226 930; www.miradordelpayne.com). Camping Río Serrano (www.horseridingpatagonia.com), about 6km S of the CONAF office, will pick guests up from the CONAF office.

The section of the route to Mirador Lago Toro is a short, relatively easy hike to a viewpoint above the road N of the Puente Weber – though it's steep in places and can get very windy on top. The walk can be turned into a considerably longer itinerary by continuing to Laguna Verde, a moderately sized lake with good views of the Paine massif, with a reasonable chance of seeing Guanaco and other wildlife on the way. The length of the route (4hrs each way from Mirador Lago Toro) means you'll almost certainly need to split it over two days, however, and the only accommodation at Laguna Verde is the somewhat expensive Hostería Mirador del Paine (part of an old *estancia*, El Lazo). There's also a CONAF national park office at Laguna Verde (you'll need to have your national park entry tickets with you if asked to show them, since this is one of the entrances to the national park).

From just N of the bend in the road on the NE side of **Puente Weber**, a marked footpath branches off to the right. This leads uphill, becoming steeper before reaching a plateau. From the plateau turn right and ascend (rocky, unmarked) to **Mirador Lago Toro**, less than 1hr from the road, with fine views. Descend by the same route.

For those continuing from Mirador Lago Toro to Laguna Verde, descend to the trail on the plateau, from where the trail ascends slightly and heads NE and E over scrub and steppe and patchy forest (keep an eye out for Guanaco on the way), passing just to the S of **Laguna Honda** to reach **Laguna Verde** (4hrs from Mirador Lago Toro). Return by the same route.

Hostería Mirador del Paine is not on the bus route from Puerto Natales. However, if you can arrange transport to the *hostería*, it would be possible to start this walk from there and then continue from the Weber Bridge to the CONAF Administración office and the beginning of the Circuit (Walk 1).

Cuernos del Paine viewed across Lago Pehoé

WALK 6
Mirador Cóndor

Start/Finish	Near Camping Pehoé
Distance	3km
Rating	easy
Time	1hr 45mins (return)
Maximum altitude	200m
Map	CONAF Parque Nacional Torres del Paine (**Note** Mirador Cóndor is marked as Mirador Pehoé on some maps.)
Transport	Buses between Puerto Natales and the CONAF Administración office pick up and drop off outside Camping Pehoé and Hotel Explora.
Accommodation	Camping Pehoé (tel 02 196 0377; main office in Punta Arenas tel 061 2249 581; www.campingpehoe.com).

This is a short hike from very close to Camping Pehoé, for those staying in this area, to the viewpoint at Mirador Cóndor, overlooking Lago Pehoé.

A trail heads E up the hillside from just N of Camping Pehoé to reach Mirador Cóndor in 1hr, from where there are good views over Lago Pehoé to the Paine massif, including the Cuernos and Cerro Paine Grande. Descend by the same route.

Guanaco

WALK 7
Río Pingo and Mirador Zapata

Start/Finish	Guardería Lago Grey
Distance	33km
Duration	2–3 days
Maps	See sketch maps and free CONAF map of the national park.
Transport	Getting to the start of the trek is somewhat difficult unless you are staying at Hostería Lago Grey – in which case a transfer to the *hostería*, from the CONAF office on Lago Toro, is included in the price. Otherwise, you can arrange a shuttle from the CONAF Administración on Lago Toro to Hostería Lago Grey for around $10,000 per person one way; or it's about a 17.5km walk. Guardería Lago Grey is just a short distance along the road from Hostería Lago Grey.
Accommodation	Two unserviced campsites, Campamento Pingo and Campamento Zapata; there's also Hostería Lago Grey (tel 061 2712 100, www.turismolagogrey.com) at the beginning of the trek. See Appendix B for a full list of huts and campsites.

This short two or three-day trek on the western side of the national park sees far fewer visitors than the various sections of the Circuit and the 'W', and is thus a good place to see wildlife – including Torrent Ducks and, just possibly, the elusive Huemúl. (If you do see a Huemúl, CONAF ask that you report the sighting to one of their Administration offices.) It is a fairly straightforward walk, largely through forest, with two unserviced campsites. The route provides views of the awe-inspiring Glaciar Zapata, on the edge of the Campo de Hielo Sur. The mosquitoes, however, can be ferocious. While you're in the area, there are two short walks from near Hostería Lago Grey (see sketch map) – a trail N from Guardería Lago Grey to the S shore of Lago Grey, and another which climbs steeply S to Mirador Ferrier. ▸

There has been discussion of making it compulsory to hire a registered guide for the Mirador Zapata trek and register your visit with CONAF – check with the national park office.

The mountains above the Río Pingo from across Lago Grey

STAGE 1
Guardería Lago Grey – Campamento Zapata

Start	Guardería Lago Grey
Distance	13.5km
Rating	easy–moderate
Time	4hrs
Maximum altitude	260m
Map	CONAF Parque Nacional Torres del Paine
Accommodation	Campamento Pingo; Campamento Zapata; Hostería Lago Grey (tel 061 2712 100, www.turismolagogrey.com)

From **Guardería Lago Grey** head NW on the true right bank of the Río Pingo, passing **Campamento Pingo** (unserviced, free) after about 30mins. The trail continues mainly through forest, passing a trail up to the right to a **viewpoint** overlooking Cascada Pingo, to reach **Campamento Zapata** (unserviced, free), 4hrs from the Guardería.

It is no longer possible to get to **Lago Pingo** (although the route is still shown on some maps), as the bridge was washed away a few years ago.

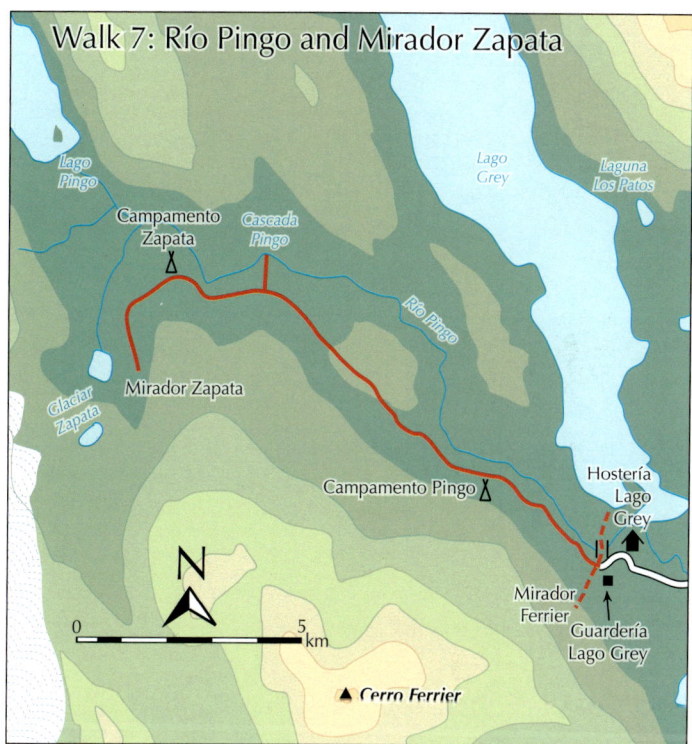

STAGE 2

Campamento Zapata – Mirador Zapata (return)

Start	Campamento Zapata
Distance	6km
Rating	moderate
Time	3hrs (return)
Maximum altitude	240m
Map	CONAF Parque Nacional Torres del Paine
Accommodation	Campamento Pingo; Campamento Zapata

From **Campamento Zapata** continue SW a further 1hr 30mins up to **Mirador Zapata,** where there are fine views of the Zapata glacier, part of the same arm of the South Patagonian Ice Field which swings down into the Tyndall and Geikie glaciers. Descend to **Campamento Zapata** by the same route.

STAGE 3
Campamento Zapata – Guardería Lago Grey

Start	Campamento Zapata
Distance	13.5km
Rating	easy–moderate
Time	4hrs
Maximum altitude	260m
Map	CONAF Parque Nacional Torres del Paine
Accommodation	Campamento Pingo; Campamento Zapata; Hostería Lago Grey (061 2712 100, www.turismolagogrey.com)

Return to Guardería Lago Grey by the same route.

Bridge near Laguna Amarga

OTHER WALKS WITHIN THE NATIONAL PARK

Laguna Amarga – Portería Sarmiento, 14km return

A trail south from the national park ticket office at Laguna Amarga takes you past Laguna Blanquillos and Laguna Los Flamencos, before arriving at the road at Portería Sarmiento and Laguna los Juncos – with a good chance of seeing flamingos and other birdlife, as well as Guanaco, on the way. Allow 90mins each way.

See Torres del Paine national park map, pp 10–11, for both these walks.

Laguna Azul and trail to Lago Dickson, 56km return

Laguna Azul is a moderately sized lake in the north-east of the national park, with a serviced campsite (tel 061 2411 157; or contact Baquedano Zamora, Baquedano 534, Puerto Natales, tel 061 2613 531) on its eastern shore. There are lovely views across the lake to the eastern peaks of the Paine massif, with the towers clearly visible. It was near Laguna Azul that a fire broke out in 2005, from a camp stove, engulfing a huge tract of land over several days before it could be brought under control. Some areas still remain scarred from this.

Take the road leading north to Laguna Azul – a little way back towards Laguna Amarga from the national park ticket office   and follow a footpath that takes you off the road for some of the way (allow a good 4hrs if walking). The road (but not the footpath) passes a waterfall on the Río Paine, Cascada Paine. As well as a good chance of seeing Lesser Rhea, there are very good, unrestricted views of the Paine massif from the road and trail.

From the campsite at Laguna Azul it is possible to follow a trail along the northern shore of the lake, then northwest past Laguna Cebolla ('onion lake') and over the Río Diente to reach **Lago Paine**. The trail then continues around the northern shore of Lago Paine, crossing the Río de los Caiquenes, then leads west to **Lago**

Dickson. Being set back further from the mountains than the Circuit, this route does give some enhanced views of the Paine massif, and, of course, there will be far fewer people on the trail. However, you won't be able to get to Refugio Dickson and thus connect this route to the Circuit trail – both lie on the opposite shore of the lake – unless you can arrange for a boat to pick you up. Some sections of the route follow a 4WD track. You'd need to allow one and a half days to get to Lago Dickson; or it would be possible to hike from the campsite at Laguna Azul as far as Laguna Cebolla and back in a day (allow 8hrs return).

EXCURSIONS FROM PUERTO NATALES

Excursion 1: Cueva del Milodón

See location map, p13.

Monumento Natural Cueva del Milodón (the Milodon Cave), which lies about 22km north of Puerto Natales on the as yet unsealed road to Lago Toro in the south of Torres del Paine national park, is one of the most important archaeological sites in southern Chile.

The Cueva del Milodón is thought to have been one of the earliest sites in the region to be inhabited by Paleoindian peoples, some 9000–12,000 years ago, at

Cueva del Milodón

which time the shore of Seno Ultima Esperanza (Last Hope Sound), would have been much closer to the cave than at present. Various pits at the back of the cave support this, and arrow heads were discovered in the adjacent Cuevo del Medio. A piece of skin from an extinct giant sloth or Milodón (*Milodon darwin*) – of which there is a large model at the entrance to the cave, and at the entrance to Puerto Natales – was found here. Bones and teeth of various other species, including Dwarf Horse (*Hippidion saldiasi*) and Sabre-toothed Tiger were also discovered, and are now displayed at the Museo Regional de Magallanes in Punta Arenas. The cave was 'discovered' by Hermann Eberhard in the 1890s, and Otto Nordenskjöld was here in 1895. Later, others returned to collect more fragments of skin, using methods including dynamiting the cave floor – an endeavour in which Charley Milwall, great-uncle of Bruce Chatwin, had a famous hand.

The site consists of the main cave (Cueva Grande), two smaller caves to the southeast (Cueva del Medio and Cueva Chica), and the prominent rock formation known as Silla del Diablo ('the Devil's seat'), located close to the road (on the right when driving to the cave from Puerto Natales). A circular trail heads north from the car park to the main cave and a viewpoint; another trail heads

'The Devil's seat', Cueva del Milodón

southeast to Cueva del Medio, Cueva Chica and the Silla del Diablo.

There is no public transport to the site (buses to Torres del Paine use the sealed road further east, although some private tours to the national park travel this way from Puerto Natales), so you'll need to either join a tour (most agencies in Puerto Natales offer this) or to have your own transport. The site is open daily, 8am–9pm during summer, reduced hours in winter; entrance tickets cost $3000.

Excursion 2: Balmaceda and Serrano glaciers (Bernardo O'Higgins national park)

See location map, p13.

A two-hour trip by catamaran from Puerto Natales, at the far end of Seno Ultima Esperanza, the Balmaceda glacier spews out from between black, mist-clad crags, a mass of blue ice bristling with ice towers. Not far away, the Serrano glacier tumbles into a small bay, shedding icebergs from its snout. This whole area forms part of the enormous Bernardo O'Higgins national park – which

Balmaceda glacier and Last Hope Sound, Bernardo O'Higgins national park

covers some 35,000km^2, most of it accessible only by boat or helicopter.

Most agencies in Puerto Natales organize excursions to the Balmaceda and Serrano glaciers, or you can book a place on the boat yourself (see Appendix A). There are two operators, Turismo 21 de Mayo (Eberhard 560; tel 061 2614 420; www.turismo21demayo.cl) and Fiordos del Sur (operated by Turismo Runner, Eberhard 555; tel 061 2712 132). The latter is a faster catamaran service. In both cases, departure is dependent on weather conditions – in high winds, neither will run.

The catamaran stops at various points on its way up Last Hope Sound, including some cliffs with a colony of Blue-eyed Cormorants, and possibly again if any seals are spotted. After a brief stop near the snout of the Balmaceda glacier, with enough time to take some photos from the back of the catamaran, the catamaran continues to a landing stage, from where it is a 15min walk to a point overlooking the snout of the Serrano glacier.

There is a small CONAF office at the landing point, as well as a small campsite and toilets. Some of the private operators visiting the Balmaceda and Serrano glaciers include a trip in a zodiac in their itinerary, which gets you even closer to the glacier.

From the jetty and CONAF information kiosk follow the clear, marked trail which heads off around the shore towards the Serrano glacier – it's about 15mins to the furthest viewpoint. Keep an eye out for Condors soaring around the surrounding crags. Return to the jetty by the same route.

Excursion 3: Sierra Baguales

Sierra Baguales is a remote and little-known area northeast of Torres del Paine national park, on the border with Argentina. Red-brown cliffs frown above lush green, rolling hills, and rivers meander through stony valleys like silver snakes. A series of wild-looking rock formations runs along a ridge-top, leaning at a precarious angle – rather like a Giant's Causeway stacked on its side – and

the landscape is scattered with fossil remains and traces of petrified forest.

There is no public transport, and the whole area lies on private land, so it is very little visited – currently only two companies organize excursions here, and since it's not at the top of most people's must-see list, even these remain comparatively infrequent. There are no trails in the area and no detailed maps.

It is a measure of how few people visit the area that the Guanaco are still relatively unaccustomed to seeing humans – when we walked up a valley, a small,

Río Baguales

inquisitive group of them shadowed our progress on the opposite side, stopping whenever we did and calling frequently. There is plenty of scope for seeing other wildlife too – from Condors and Lesser Rhea to Patagonian Grey Fox and the less common Chimango Caracara.

It is thought that the Verlika pass at the head of the main valley in Sierra Baguales was used for access by the first indigenous inhabitants – the Tehuelche – who crossed into the area from further north. There is a large cave near the pass, where obsidian tools and other archaeological finds have been unearthed. *Baguales* means 'wild horses' in Tehuelche.

Slightly to the west of, and running parallel to Río Baguales, is another remote, hidden valley, that of the Río de las Chinas, which stretches northeast from Laguna Azul. The Río Baguales flows south, joining the Río de las Chinas before flowing into the eastern shore of Lago Toro.

If you travelled to Puerto Natales from El Calafate on the bus, the long, low range of mountains seen on the right after regaining the sealed road – including the prominent Cerro Tridente – lies along the Chilean-Argentine border, with the valley of the Río Baguales on the far side.

At present, if you want to visit Sierra Baguales, you will need to either join an organized trip (www. remotahotel.com or www.thesingular.com) or hire your own transport. In the latter case, you will still need to stop at the gendarme post by Estancia Cerro Guido to let them know where you are going, and just as importantly, you'll need to get permission from the landowners as you pass by Estancia Los Leones (at least basic Spanish required for both). Obviously it is essential that you respect the fact that you're on someone's private land – close all gates on the road behind you and do not try to camp.

If you are driving, turn right off the road to Torres del Paine before Laguna Amarga, drive north then northeast on an unsealed road, passing Estancia Cerro Guido and a small checkpoint (where you will be expected to stop and

Sierra Baguales

explain where you are going), before turning north again and entering the valley of the Río Baguales, with the buttresses of a range of mountains, including Cerro Tridente (actually in Argentina), on your right. Pass by Estancia Los Leones – you are on their private land, and should have their permission to drive through here – making sure you close any gates behind you. Lying beyond the mountains at the distant head of the valley, almost due north, is Lago Argentina and El Calafate.

Tours will probably stop about halfway up the valley, roughly opposite a huge, prominent white boulder on the opposite (east) side of the valley. Heading west and ascending alongside a fence (on its north side) brings you out onto open tops, where you can follow the bizarre, lopsided rock formations which stretch along the ridges. Either return along the same route, or cut across more shallow valleys heading roughly east before descending to the 4WD track.

Hikers below rock formations in Sierra Baguales

LOS GLACIARES NATIONAL PARK, ARGENTINA

On the trail to Cerro Torre (Walk 8)

It doesn't take much more than a cursory look at a map of southern Patagonia to see just how close Torres del Paine is to Los Glaciares national park in Argentina – some 25km as the crow flies from the N side of Torres del Paine – where the great attractions are the spectacular trekking in the Cerro Fitzroy (El Chaltén) area, and the vast expanse of the Perito Moreno glacier (one of the world's few non-retreating glaciers). Agencies in Puerto Natales organize day trips to the Perito Moreno glacier (tel 061 2411 858, www.servitur.cl), and for those with more time there are buses from Puerto Natales to El Calafate (5hrs), from where there are frequent buses (3hrs 30mins) to El Chaltén, the start of hikes to see Cerro Torre and Cerro Fitzroy.

Visas are not required for UK, US and most European nationals travelling to Argentina. There is a national park entrance fee for those visiting the Perito Moreno glacier, payable at the park entrance as you drive from El Calafate. However there is currently no national park fee payable for the Fitzroy (El Chaltén) area of Los Glaciares national park (although introducing one has been discussed in the past). Instead, all buses arriving in El Chaltén are first

ARGENTINA AT A GLANCE	
Country name	Republic of Argentina (República Argentina)
Capital	Buenos Aires
Language	Spanish
Currency	Argentine Peso (ARS)
Exchange rate	£1=ARS20.94, €1=ARS16.39, US$1=ARS14.28; ARS1=£0.05, €0.06 or US$0.07.
Population	40,120,000 (2010 census)
Time zone	GMT-2 (October–March), GMT-3 (April–September)
International dialling code	+54
Internet country code	.ar
Electricity	220V/50 (two-pin, flat rather than round as in Chile)

diverted to the national park office, where visitors attend a short introduction to the area and an explanation of what you can, and can't, do in the national park.

The best map for trekking in the Fitzroy area of Argentina's Los Glaciares national park is 'Monte Fitz Roy & Cerro Torre Trekking–Mountaineering Minimap' (Zagier & Urruty, 1:50,000, 100m contour lines).

Excursion from El Calafate

Excursion 4: Perito Moreno glacier

Transport

Taxis from El Calafate to the Perito Moreno glacier cost around $US40, which includes the return journey and a 1hr waiting time at the glacier. There's a taxi office next to the bus station in El Calafate, and most agencies in town also run excursions there. Buses between El Calafate and Puerto Natales get fully booked in the summer, so try to get your ticket at least a day in advance, if possible (the same applies to buses to/from El Chaltén). If you're visiting the glacier from Puerto Natales, several agencies operate day trips (see Appendix A).

Accommodation

There is plenty of accommodation in El Calafate. Try Los Dos Piños (9 de Julio 358, tel 02902 491 271, www.losdospinos.com); Marco Polo Inn (Los Lagos 82, www.marcopoloinncalafate.com) is a large, popular hostel on the E side of town. There is a good range of accommodation listed on www.losglaciares.com and www.calafate.com.

The Perito Moreno glacier, a UNESCO World Heritage Site and one of the world's few non-retreating glaciers, is a spectacular site, spilling down off the South Patagonian Ice Field to shed enormous chunks of ice, right under your nose, into Lago Argentino.

It's about 15mins walk from the car park down to the various lookout points opposite the snout of the glacier.

Perito Moreno glacier

WALK 8
Cerro Fitzroy (El Chaltén) and Cerro Torre

Start/Finish	El Chaltén
Distance	38.5km
Duration	3–4 days (plus a further 1 day if following the extension, Stage 4)
Maps	See sketch maps and Monte Fitz Roy & Cerro Torre Trekking–Mountaineering Minimap.
Transport	Cal-Tur (Av. Liberador 1080, El Calafate, tel 02902 491 368, www.caltur.com.ar) and Chaltén Travel (Av. Liberador 1174, El Calafate, tel 02902 492 212, www.chaltentravel.com) both operate two bus services a day between El Calafate and El Chaltén, one around 7.30am and another around 6.00pm, with a further service around 1pm during high season (3hrs 30mins). Book tickets in advance if possible, as seats do sell out.
Accommodation	Camping within the **national park** is permitted only at these unserviced sites: Campamento Agostini (also called Campamento Jim Bridwell and Campamento Laguna Torre), Campamento Poincenot, Campamento Laguna Capri and Refugio Los Troncos (on the extension, Stage 4). The latter is on private land and costs around US$5 to stay; the others are free. There's also a hut at Refugio Los Troncos (around US$15). There's quite a good range of accommodation in **El Chaltén**, although budget digs tend to fill up fast, so book ahead if you can. Highly recommended is Condor de los Andes (Av. Río de las Vueltas y Halvorsen, tel 02962 493 101, www.condordelosandes.com), on the SE side of town; otherwise try Albergue Patagonia (Av. San Martín 493, tel 02962 493 019, www.elchalten.com/patagonia) and Aylen-Aike (Trevisán 125, tel 02962 493 317, www.elchalten.com/aylenaike), or the more upmarket Hostería El Puma (Lionel Terray 212, tel 02962 493 095, www.hosteriaelpuma.com.ar). See www.elchalten.com.

Along with Torres del Paine national park, the Fitzroy area of Argentina's Los Glaciares national park is unquestionably the most popular trekking area in Patagonia, and deservedly so. This outstanding 3–4 day trek allows you to get surprisingly close to both Cerro Fitzroy and Cerro Torre on clear, easy trails, with first-rate views. Cerro Fitzroy (sometimes called Monte Fitzroy, and often spelled Fitz Roy) is also known as El Chaltén in Tehuelche – meaning 'the smoking one', on account of the plume of cloud usually seen trailing from its summit.

The national park office is on the left as you drive into El Chaltén from El Calafate (tel 02962 493 004; www. losglaciares.com) – everyone stops in here to be given a short presentation on the park and, in no uncertain terms, the rules and regulations trekkers are expected to follow. In contrast to Torres del Paine, there are no large huts or hotels within the national park. Camping is at designated sites only. If you don't want to camp you can stay in one of the many hotels and *hostales* in El Chaltén (the nearest town, named after the peak) and make day trips from there. This policy has benefitted the national park by preserving it in a somewhat wilder, less developed state than Torres del Paine.

A few years ago the section of the route from Campamento Agostini to Campamento Poincenot (Stage 2) was closed to prevent erosion. Although open at the time of writing, if it closes again, trekkers would have to backtrack to El Chaltén then follow the route to Campamento Poincenot (Stage 5) in reverse.

STAGE 1
El Chaltén – Campamento Agostini

Start	El Chaltén
Distance	9.5km
Rating	easy–moderate
Time	3hrs
Maximum altitude	630m
Map	Monte Fitz Roy & Cerro Torre Trekking–Mountaineering Minimap
Accommodation	Campamento Agostini (also called Campamento Jim Bridwell)

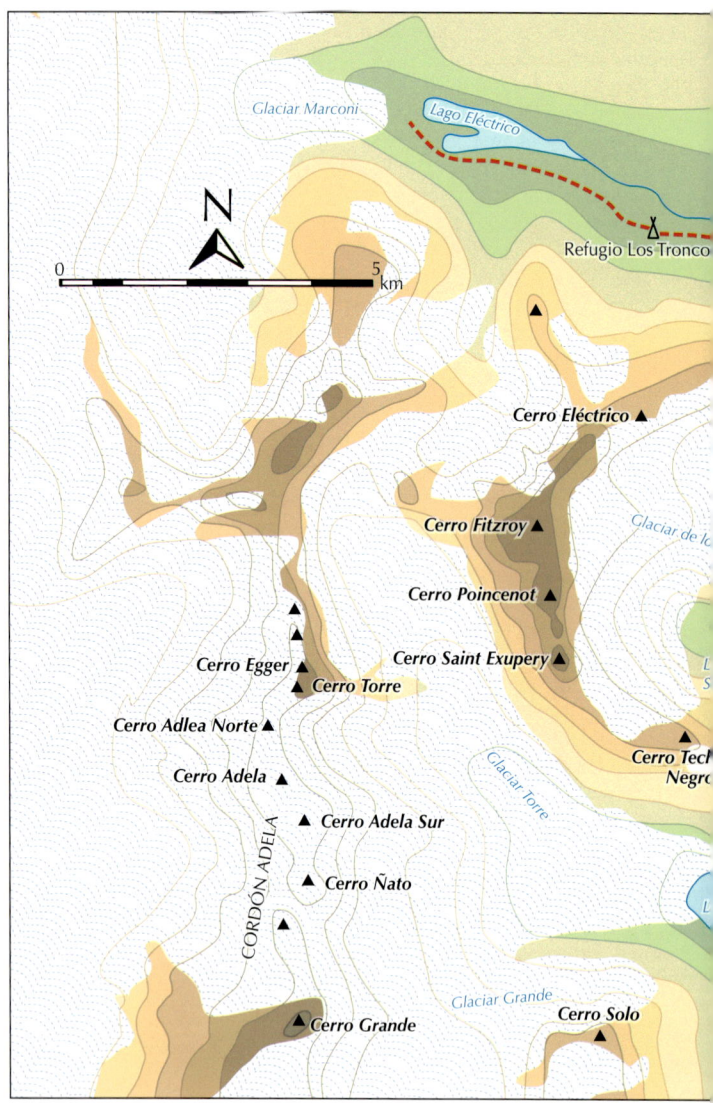

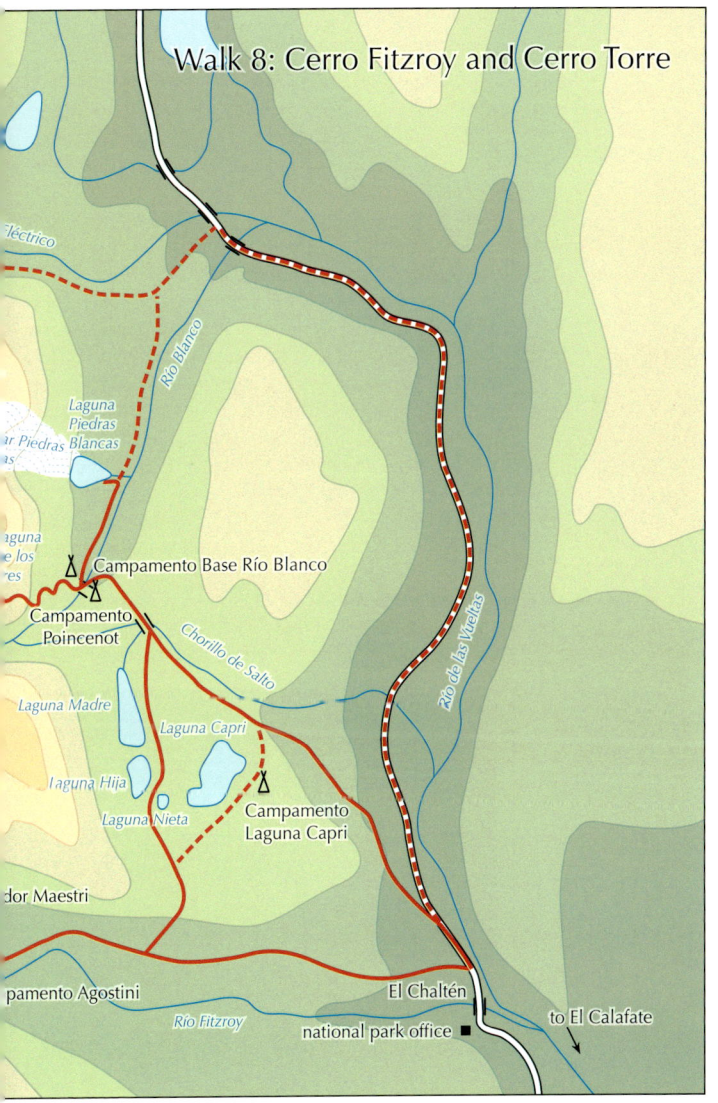

Walk 8: Cerro Fitzroy and Cerro Torre

An easy walk to one of the most spectacular mountain views anywhere in the Patagonian Andes – of the iconic, slender finger of rock that is Cerro Torre and the Cordón Adela.

Walk N along the main road in **El Chaltén**, away from the bus station and the national park office, and turn left (W) onto a marked trail. Ascend over a slight rise, passing a skeletal, burnt tree with a sign reading 'Monument to a careless trekker'. Continue with good views ahead of Cerro Solo, passing a trail coming in from the left (and a sign reminding trekkers that burning toilet paper causes forest fires), and ascending to arrive at Mirador Laguna Torre, a saddle with fine views to Cerro Torre ahead.

Continue, descending slightly and passing a **marked trail** on your right to Laguna Madre and Laguna Hija (see Stage 2, below) and later another marked 'prestadores de sevicios' (equipment hire). After skirting to the right of a marshy area, and crossing flats close to the Río Fitzroy, the trail ascends over the high moraine bank ahead to arrive amid a jumbled rocky wilderness where you'll find **Campamento Agostini** sheltered under the trees.

'Monument to a careless trekker' – burnt tree near El Chaltén, on the trail to Cerro Torre

Campamento Agostini is a simple but pleasant unserviced site, with water from a hose, and a toilet back among the moraine debris.

Once you've pitched your tent, head up onto the moraine for sensational views out across Laguna Torre to the needle-like finger of Cerro Torre, alongside the Cordón Adela and the Torre glacier. Following the moraine ridge around to the right (NW) will bring you to up to Mirador Maestri and more views.

Don't try crossing the Río Fitzroy below the lake – it's extremely dangerous.

STAGE 2
Campamento Agostini – Campamento Poincenot

Start	Campamento Agostini
Distance	10km
Rating	easy–moderate
Time	3hrs 30mins
Maximum altitude	750m
Map	Monte Fitz Roy & Cerro Torre Trekking–Mountaineering Minimap
Accommodation	Campamento Agostini (also called Campamento Jim Bridwell), Campamento Poincenot

A pleasant route through forest then alongside and above Laguna Madre, with increasingly spectacular views of Cerro Fitz Roy and its satellite peaks. A few years ago the trail here was closed to prevent erosion. In this case, the only option is to return to El Chaltén and follow the route to Campamento Poincenot (Stage 5) in reverse.

From **Campamento Agostini**, backtrack down the valley of the Río Fitzroy, then turn left on the **trail** marked

Cerro Torre across Laguna Torre

Laguna Madre and Laguna Hija. Ascend through forest, keeping an eye out for Magellenic woodpeckers, crossing a saddle and then descending, and passing a **trail** on your right to Laguna Capri and Campamento Laguna Capri.

Keep straight ahead, passing between **Laguna Hija** and **Laguna Nieta** to arrive at the rather idyllic S shore of **Laguna Madre**. This makes a perfect spot for lunch, with good views N over the lake to the high peaks beyond. *Madre* means 'mother' in Spanish, *hija* and *nieta* 'daughter' and 'niece' respectively – as implied by the relative sizes of the lakes.

The trail climbs gradually above the E shore of Laguna Madre, then descends again and passes alongside a marshy area with spectacular views of Cerro Fitzroy beyond, before meeting the main **path from El Chalten**. Turn left onto this, crossing a small bridge over the Chorrillo del Salto and then finally veering left to arrive at **Campamento Poincenot**, sheltered under the trees.

Campamento Poincenot is a large, simple unserviced campsite under the trees near the Río Blanco, and makes a perfect base for visiting Laguna de los Tres and Laguna Piedras Blancas.

STAGE 3

Campamento Poincenot – Laguna de los Tres
(return)

Start	Campamento Poincenot
Distance	5km
Rating	moderate
Time	3hrs (return)
Maximum altitude	approx. 1200m
Map	Monte Fitz Roy & Cerro Torre Trekking–Mountaineering Minimap
Accommodation	Campamento Poincenot

A short, stiff climb to the viewpoint at Laguna de los Tres, with astounding close-up views of Cerro Fitzroy.

Head W from **Campamento Poincenot**, crossing the bridge over the Río Blanco and several braided channels. Pass a **trail on the right** which follows the Río Blanco (this trail is part of Stage 4), then ascend gradually, passing **Campamento Base Río Blanco**, a bivouac used by climbers (trekkers are not allowed to sleep here).

Continue ascending, the route clearly visible ahead of you, and reach a rocky shelf. Cross this before ascending again over boulders and scree. At the top of the moraine you gain sudden and spectacular views of the huge, towering bulk of Cerro Fitzroy across **Laguna de los Tres**.

For good views of **Laguna Sucia** head left around the SW edge of Laguna de los Tres, scrambling up over the raised ground beyond, to a point where you can peer down into the lake. Laguna Sucia sits hemmed in by sheer cliffs, down which fragments of glacier occasionally tumble.

Cerro Fitzroy across Laguna de los Tres

Return to **Campamento Poincenot** by the same route.

STAGE 4
Campamento Poincenot –
Laguna Piedras Blancas (return)

Start	Campamento Poincenot
Distance	5km
Rating	moderate
Time	2hrs 30mins
Maximum altitude	680m
Map	Monte Fitz Roy & Cerro Torre Trekking–Mountaineering Minimap
Accommodation	Campamento Poincenot

A short, half-day excursion to one of the most spectacular glaciers in the area. An early start should give you enough time to complete this excursion before returning to El Chalten the same day (see Stage 5). Alternatively, it is possible to make an extension to the route by continuing along the Río Blanco (route less clear) to the Río Eléctrico and Refugio Los Troncos. After an overnight stop at the *refugio,* return along the valley of the Río Electrico to the main road and follow this S to El Chaltén.

From **Campamento Poincenot**, cross the Río Blanco as in Stage 3, then turn right and follow the trail alongside the river's true left bank. After about 45mins you arrive at a side-valley and the outflow stream from Laguna Piedras Blancas. Turn left, following the valley and scrambling over huge boulders (care needed here – watch out for rock fall from above) to reach the E shore of **Laguna Piedras Blancas**, with the enormous icefall of the Piedras Blancas glacier beyond, bristling with ice towers.

Piedras Blancas glacier

From Laguna Piedras Blancas either return to **Campamento Poincenot** by the same route or extend the route by continuing N then following the valley of the Río Eléctrico to Refugio Los Troncos, as described below.

Extension to Río Eléctrico and Refugio Los Troncos

The following route continues down the Río Blanco to the Río Eléctrico and Refugio Los Troncos (3hrs), with a night there before returning to El Chaltén along the valley of the Río Eléctrico and the main road (5hrs) (of course, you could also return to Campamento Poincenot, and continue from there as in Stage 5).

Those who plan to continue to Refugio Los Troncos will need to cross the outlet stream from **Laguna Piedras Blancas**. There is no bridge, but it should be possible to ford the outlet stream or boulder-hop if the water is not too high. Cross carefully, using a stick or walking poles for support, or linking arms with fellow trekkers. Continue above the true left bank of the **Río Blanco**, guided by the occasional cairn, ascending sometimes and with some slightly exposed sections.

About 1hr beyond the side-valley leading to Laguna Piedras Blancas you meet up with a much clearer trail heading up the **valley of the Río Eléctrico**. Turn left onto this, crossing grassland and following the upper reaches of the Río Eléctrico, to reach **Refugio Los Troncos** in a further 2hrs (camping, some basic chalet-style huts and minimal supplies). The campsite sits in the shelter of Piedra del Fraile, a huge erratic boulder dumped here by glaciers.

Return to El Chaltén by following the Río Eléctrico downstream (E). ◄ Reach the main road by the bridge over the Río Eléctrico (3hrs); turn right and follow the road a further 2hrs into El Chaltén.

Continuing further alongside Lago Eléctrico on a faint path gives views of the wind-blasted, icy wastes of the Glaciar Marconi (up to 6hrs return).

STAGE 5
Campamento Poincenot – El Chaltén

Start	Campamento Poincenot
Distance	9km
Rating	easy
Time	2hrs 30mins
Maximum altitude	680m
Map	Monte Fitz Roy & Cerro Torre Trekking–Mountaineering Minimap
Accommodation	Campamento Poincenot. See above for El Chaltén.

A final, easy stage down to El Chaltén.

From **Campamento Poincenot**, retrace your steps to the **junction** with the trail to Laguna Madre and take the left fork to head around the edge of a marshy area. Pass the

Cerro Fitzroy from the trail SE of Campamento Poincenot

other end of the **Laguna Capri trail** on your right. Pass through areas of forest, with the Chorillo del Salto stream on your left, before gradually descending above the Río de las Vueltas and passing an enormous boulder on your left. Continue descending to join the road to **El Chaltén** and arrive back in **town** 2hrs 30mins from Campamento Poincenot.

Old fishing boats, Puerto Natales

PUERTO NATALES

Puerto Natales, a quiet and exceptionally pleasant little town on the shore of Seno Ultima Esperanza (Last Hope Sound), is effectively the 'gateway' to Torres del Paine national park. Although most visitors pass through here only briefly on their way to or from the national park, you are strongly encouraged to spend a little extra time here.

There are plenty of possible day trips, notably to Cueva del Milodón; the Balmaceda and Serrano glaciers; and the remote Sierra Baguales (see 'Excursions from Puerto Natales' for all three trips). There's also Puerto Bories, site of the old freezer plant (Frigerífico Bories) – upon the fortunes of which the town of Puerto Natales largely grew into being, in the days before tourism. Established in 1915, the plant processed some 300,000 sheep per year at its peak, and was finally closed in 1993. Puerto Bories lies about 2km northwest of Puerto Natales on shore of Last Hope Sound, and part of the complex is now open as a museum.

Puerto Natales

Accommodation
1 Casa Cecilia
2 Erratic Rock 1
3 Hostal Dickson
4 Hotel Lady Florence Dixie
5 Hostal Nancy
6 Hostal Francis Drake
7 Hostal Dos Lagunas
8 Hostel Natales
9 Hostal Patagonia Adventure
10 The Singing Lamb
11 Hostal Amerindia
12 Pine Mapu Cottage B&B
13 Casa Lucy
14 Hostal Lily Patagonicos
15 Last Hope Hostel
16 We Are Patagonia B&B
17 Yaganhouse Hostel
18 Erratic Rock 2
19 Hostal Chorrillos
20 Hotel Remota
21 The Singular

Restaurants & cafes
22 Pastelería Lily
23 Luchito
24 El Bote
25 Marítimo
26 Mesita Grande
27 El Asador
28 El Living
29 Restaurant Oveja Negra
30 La Casa de Pepe

31 Café and Books
32 Coffee Planet
33 Restaurant Ultima Esperanza
34 Café Kaiken
35 Aldea
36 Cafetería Cangrejo Rojo
37 Chocolatería Patagonia Dulce

Transport
38 Bus-Sur
39 Taxi Milodon
40 Pacheco
41 Herz
42 Turismo Zaahj
43 Buses Gomez
44 Buses Fernández
45 Navimag & Comapa
46 Radio Taxi Natales
47 Rodoviario bus station & Turismo Zaahj
48 Navimag

Agencies
49 Erratic Rock 1
50 Patagonia Adventure
51 Baquedano Zamora
52 Servitur
53 Turismo 21 de Mayo

Banks, ATMs & exchange offices
54 Banco Estado
55 Banco de Chile

56 Bank Santander
57 Cambios Latino Americana
58 Cambios Milly

Other
59 Torres del Paine
60 Fruit & vegetable shops
61 Dried fruit shop
62 Supermarket
63 Laundrette
64 Copec petrol station
65 Craft market
66 Nandú Artesan
67 Mirriam Parra
68 Pharmacy
69 JL Computacion
70 Nethouse Cybercafé
71 Post office

158

It's also worth wandering down to the old boat yard, a wonderfully colourful, jumbled mass of old fishing boats, some still in service, others part sunk – all bright and peeling paintwork in the afternoon sun.

Accommodation

There is no shortage of places to stay in Puerto Natales, ranging from the basic to the luxurious, although they are mostly in the mid-range bracket. Unless otherwise specified, rates are for high season; some of the places that open all year drop their rates considerably in low season.

Casa Cecilia
Tomás Rogers 60
tel 061 2412 698
www.casaceciliahostal.com
Excellent *residencial*, and one of the nicest places to stay in Puerto Natales. Friendly and informative, with spotless rooms (shared and private bathrooms) set on two floors around a pleasant communal area, exceptionally good breakfasts, internet access, luggage storage, equipment hire. Deservedly popular, so book well in advance. Rates: dbl/twin $54,000, single $51,000 (private bathroom); dbl/twin $34,000, single $22,000 (shared bathroom)

Erratic Rock
Baquedano 719
www.erraticrock.com
Popular place with dorms and single/double rooms with shared /private bathrooms. Rates: dorm $15,000;

dbl $32,000 (shared bathroom) or $35,000 (private bathroom)

Hostal Dos Lagunas
Barros Arana 104
tel 061 2415 133
doslagunas@hotmail.com
Excellent value, one of the best budget options in town. Rates: dbl/twin $25,000, single $18,000, shared (up to 5 people) $10,000 per person

Hostal Patagonia Adventure
Tomás Rogers 179
tel 061 2411 028
www.apatagonia.com
Very nice (and popular – book ahead) place on the main square, with double/twin rooms and a dorm, a good restaurant and equipment hire. Rates: dbl/twin $25,000, dorm $10,000

Hotel Remota
Ruta 9 Norte, km 1.5, Huerto 279
tel 061 2414 040
bookings tel 02 2387 1500
www.remotahotel.com
Remota offers fully inclusive packages for 3–7 nights (dbl 3 nights US$1800–US$2250 per person) – for which you get an unrivalled range of inclusive excursions, delicious meals (breakfast, lunch and dinner, including wine, and packed lunches for excursions), luxurious rooms and service, airport transfers to Punta Arenas and the use of spa and sauna room – meaning that it does actually represent quite good value. One of the great attractions of Remota is the fact that it is in Puerto Natales

and not in the national park itself – consider the environmental as well as the scenic impact of allowing large hotel complexes to be built within the national park. Remota often offers discounted packages (with prices dropping by up to 30%)

Hostal Dickson
Bulnes 307
tel 061 2411 871
www.hostaldickson.net
Lovely *residential* – clean, friendly and well priced

The Singing Lamb
Arauco 779
tel 061 2410 958
www.thesinginglamb.com
New, eco-friendly hostel with dorms as well as dbls with private bathroom

Hostal Amerindia
Barros Arana 135
tel 061 411 945
www.hostelamerindia.com
New hostal offering dbls with shared and private bathrooms

Pire Mapu Cottage B&B
Esmeralda 1435
tel 061 2415 176
www.piremapucottage.com
Cottage-style B&B

Other accommodation in Puerto Natales includes:

Casa Lucy
Miraflores 969
tel 061 2413 792
www.casalucypuertonatales.com

Hostal Chorrillos
Galvarino Esquina Chorillos 598
tel 061 2411 448
www.hostalchorrillos.cl

Hostal Francis Drake
Phillipi 383
tel 061 2411 553
www.hostalfrancisdrake.com

Hostal Nancy
Ramirez 540
tel 061 2410 022
www.nataleslodge.cl

Hostel Natales
Ladrilleros 209
tel 061 2414 731
www.hostelnatales.cl

Hotel Indigo
Ladrilleros 105
tel 061 2740 670
www.noihotels.com

Hotel Lady Florence Dixie
Bulnes 655
tel 061 2411 158
www.hotelflorencedixie.cl

Hostal Lily Patagonicos
Arturo Prat 479
tel 061 414 063
www.lilipatagonicos.com

Last Hope Hostel
Arturo Pratt 499
tel 061 2413 707
www.facebook.com/hostellasthope

The Singular
Puerto Bories
tel 061 2722 030
www.thesingular.com

We Are Patagonia B&B
Galvarino 745
tel 061 2411 191
www.wearepatagonia.com

Yaganhouse Hostel
O'Higgins 584
tel 061 2414 137
www.yaganhouse.cl

Restaurants and cafés
El Asador Patagónico
Arturo Prat 158
tel 061 2413 553
Seriously meaty Patagonian grill

El Living
Arturo Prat 156
tel 061 2411 140
www.el-living.com
Excellent vegetarian food, juices, coffee and homemade cakes

La Casa de Pepe
Tomas Rogers 131
tel 061 2410 950
Good, fairly low-key place with a good range of traditional dishes

Maritimo
(Baquedano)
Lovely down-to-earth seafood restaurant on Baquedano (not on the waterfront, as many maps still mark it) with very reasonable prices

Mesita Grande
Arturo Prat 196
tel 061 2411 571
www.mesitagrande.cl
A true Puerto Natales institution, this near-legendary pizzeria is

almost always busy – reservations recommended

Pasteleria Lily
Bulnes 481
Excellent bakery and pastry shop

Restaurant Oveja Negra
Tomás Rogers 169
Nice laid-back local on the main square

Luchito and **El Bote**
(both on Bulnes)
Two places with a cheaper than average *menu del día*

Café and Books
A nice little café with a good bookshop attached on Encalada

Café Kaiken
Baquedano 699
tel 09 8295 2036
Tiny family-run place with just a few tables, very popular

Other restaurants and cafes include:

Aldea
Barros Arana 132
tel 061 414 027

Cafeteria Cangrejo Rojo
Santiago Bueras 782
tel 061 241 2436

Chocolateria Patagonia Dulce
Barros Arana 233
tel 061 241 5285

Restaurant Ultima Esperanza
354 Eberhard
tel 061 411 391
www.restaurantuesperanza.galeon.com

The excellent restaurant at **Hotel Remota** is also open to non-guests (see above).

Transport

Most of the major **bus** companies running national routes have their offices on the eastern side of town, on or near Baquedano, or at the Rodoviario bus station on Av España. When arriving in Puerto Natales you are sometimes given the option of jumping off on Bulnes, which is closer to the Plaza than Rodoviario or the offices on Baquedano. Buses for Torres del Paine (Buses Gomez, Pacheco, Bus-Sur) pick up outside these companies' offices on Arturo Prat, near the corner of the Plaza, or from the Rodoviario bus station – check which one when you buy your tickets.

Buses Fernández
Ramirez 399/Av España 1455
tel 061 2411 111
www.busesfernandez.com

Buses Gomez
Av España 1455
tel 061 2411 971
www.busesgomez.com

Bus-Sur
Baquedano 668
tel 061 2614 221
www.bus-sur.cl

Pacheco
Ramirez 224
tel 061 2414 800
www.busespacheco.com

Turismo Zaahj
Arturo Prat 236/Av España 1455
tel 061 2411 355
www.turismozaahj.co.cl

There is a **taxi** office on Baquedano (Taxi Milodon, tel 061 2410 426). For **ferries**, the Navimag office is now at Rodoviario (Av España 1455; tel 061 2412 554; www.navimag.com). There's a **Europcar** office on Bulnes.

Agencies

Many of the hotels and hostels in Puerto Natales organize tours; in addition, there are plenty of agencies in town where you can arrange anything from an excursion to Cueva del Milodón to a trip to Los Glaciares national park in Argentina. Among the best of these is **Erratic Rock** (Baquedano 719; www.erraticrock.com), which is also a good place to go for equipment hire.

To book an excursion to the Balmaceda and Serrano glaciers, you want **Turismo 21 de Mayo** (Eberhard 560; tel 061 2614 420; www.turismo21demayo.cl). **Punta Alta** (Encalada 244; www.puntaalta.cl) offers combined catamaran/zodiac trips including to the Balmaceda and Serrano glaciers as well as the Río Serrano.

Servitur (Arturo Pratt 353; tel 061 2411 858; www.servitur.cl) runs excursions to the Milodón Cave as well as places further afield including the Peritio Moreno glacier and El Chaltén in Argentina.

Other agencies in Puerto Natales include:

Chile Nativo
Barros Arana 176
www.chilenativo.com

Patagonia Adventure
Tomás Rogers 179
www.apatagonia.com

Antares Patagonia
Barros Arana 111
www.antarespatagonia.com

Indigo
Ladrilleros 105
www.indigopatagonia.com

Fantastico Sur
Esmeralda 661
www.fantasticosur.com

Banks and ATMs
You should not rely on ATMs in Puerto Natales for all the money you need to carry with you in the national park – they frequently run out (keeping just enough for locals to use), and since you can only use credit cards at some lodges and not for transport in the park or entrance tickets, this would effectively delay your start until you can get some cash.

There are ATMs at Banco de Chile and Banco Santiago on Bulnes, Bank Santander at the corner of Bulnes and Encalada, and Banco Estado on Bories, on one side of the Plaza. There's also an ATM in the pharmacy on the corner of Bulnes and Encalada. If you are unable to withdraw money from any of the above, try the ATM at the Copec petrol station on Bulnes – often the last to run out of cash.

Exchange offices include Cambios Mily on Encalada and Cambios Latino Americana on Bulnes.

Keeping in touch
The post office is on Eberhard, on one side of the Plaza. Some hotels and *pensions* have internet access, otherwise there are Coffee Planet and Nethouse Cybercafe, both on Bulnes, and JL Computacion on the corner of Eberhard and Magallanes. You can make telephone calls from the latter; there are also call boxes on the Plaza and at other locations.

Shopping
For stocking up before a trek, there is a decent-sized supermarket on Baquedano, and two fruit and vegetable shops almost opposite. One block further along, also on Baquedano, there is an excellent little shop selling a wide range of dried fruit – perfect for hiking. There is a large, modern pharmacy on the corner of Bulnes and Encalada. For maps as well as new and second-hand books, head for Café & Books on Encalada. There are some good local craft shops, including the excellent Mirriam Parra on Bulnes and Nandú Artesan on Eberhard, and a craft market on the corner of Bernardo Philipi and Baquedano. Torres del Paine is a good local equipment manufacturer on Baquedano.

SANTIAGO

Chile's capital, Santiago, is often over-looked by those visiting Patagonia, who tend to view it as little more than a place to change planes or spend a night on the way to the mountains further south. While admittedly not as exciting a destination as Buenos Aires, it is an interesting city, in the shadow of the Andes and surrounded by vineyards, and well worth two or three days of your time on the South American continent.

Arrival

Santiago's main airport, Arturo Merino Benítez, lies about 25km northwest of the city, in the suburb of Pudahuel. Shuttle buses run into the city centre from outside the arrivals hall every 30mins or so, operated by **Tur-Bus** (www.turbus.cl) and **CentroPuerto** (www.centropuerto.cl). The most convenient stop for hotels in the city centre is Los Héroes (metro station). You can also book private transfers from the airport to your hotel, run by **TransVip** (tel 02 2677 3000; www.transvip.cl). Alternatively a **taxi** (tel 02 2601 9880; www.taxioficial.cl) from the airport to a hotel in the city centre should set you back about US$25 (allow about 25mins journey time, considerably more during rush hour).

Once in the city centre, Santiago's modern **metro** system (www.metrosantiago.cl) is reliable and easy to use. If you're planning to do a lot of travelling around in Santiago, con-sider getting a **'Tarjeta Bip!'** travel card (www.transantiago.cl). These are

available from metro ticket offices, with each single fare covering up to three interconnected metro/bus jour-neys over a period of 2hrs. **Taxi** fares are very reasonable; stick to official, metered taxis (black with a yellow roof), carry the right change and avoid paying with large denomination notes, and steer clear of unmarked cars.

If you're heading out of Santiago by **bus**, you'll need to go to either Terminal de Buses Alameda, Terminal de Buses Santiago (also known as Terminal de Estación Central) or Terminal San Borja (mainly buses heading north). The first two are close to Universidad de Santiago metro station; Terminal San Borja is closer to Estación Central metro station. There's a fourth bus terminal at Los Héroes. Trains south to Temuco leave from Estación Central.

Accommodation
Hotel Foresta
Subercaseaux 353
tel 02 2639 6261
www.forestahotel.cl
Rambling old place, full of character and very good value, in the district of Lastarria (Bellas Artes or Universidad Católica metro stations). Rooms facing onto the street or Cerro Santa Lucia are best.

Hotel Fundador
Paseo Serrano 34
tel 02 2387 1200
www.fundador.cl
Recently renovated four-star hotel, with large, comfortable rooms and courteous staff, conveniently located

in a quiet street near Universidad de Chile metro station.

Hotel Paris 813
Calle Paris 813
tel 02 2664 0921 or 02 2639 4037
www.hotelparis813.com
Clean, very good-value place, close to Universidad de Chile metro station. Ask for a room in the newer part of the hotel rather than the older wing, which has seen better days.

Hotel Paris Londres
Londres 54
tel 02 2633 9192
www.londres.cl
Popular budget option near to Universidad de Chile metro station.

Where to eat
Santiago's huge covered market, **Mercado Central** (www.mercadocentral.cl) is one of the most atmospheric places to eat seafood in the city. The best-known of the various eateries here is **Donde Augusto** (www.dondeaugusto.cl), although there are plenty of other, sometimes cheaper, places. **El Naturista** (Calle Huértanos 1046; tel 02 2696 1668; www.elnaturista.cl) is an excellent vegetarian restaurant.

What to see
While in Santiago, don't miss the opportunity to visit the **Museo Chileno de Arte Precolombino** (Bandera 361; tel 02 2928 1500; www.precolombino.cl) – without any doubt the finest museum in Chile – and

La Chascona (Fernando Márquez de la Plata 192; tel 02 2777 8741; www.fundacionneruda.org), the beautifully maintained former home of the Chilean poet Pablo Neruda. **Plaza de Armas** is a good place to start wandering, and the nearby **Mercado Central** should be visited even if you don't plan on eating there. The **Centro Cultural Palacio de la Moneda** (Alameda; www.gobiernodechile.cl) has some good exhibitions and an outstanding craft shop. For open space head for **Cerro San Cristóbal**, the long green hill and park north of Bellavista and Providencia, with its funicular and cable car.

About 120km outside Santiago is the historic port of **Valparaíso**, with its amazing warren of brightly painted houses that now constitute a UNESCO World Heritage Site. There's another of Neruda's houses here, **La Sebastiana** (Ferrari 692; tel 032 256 606; www.fundacionneruda.org), which is also open as a museum. Buses to Valparaíso depart from Santiago's Terminal Alameda, behind Estación Central. There are also plenty of **vineyards** which can be visited (including Viña Concha y Toro; tel 02 2476 5000; www.conchaytoro.com), and you're only a short drive from the **Andes** (see Dominique Argenson's *Randonnées Chiliennes* and Jim Ryan's Cicerone guide *Aconcagua* for details of short hikes around Santiago). You can even get reasonably close to **Aconcagua** in a day (Andes Wind runs full-day trips to the Horcones Valley; tel 02 2458 7411; www.andeswind.cl).

Cemetery, Punta Arenas

PUNTA ARENAS

The **airport** of Punta Arenas is located about 20km north of the town. **Shuttle buses** meet incoming flights, or it's about $6,000 for a **taxi** into town. For those in a hurry, it's also possible to get a **bus** from the airport straight to Puerto Natales – Bus-Sur (tel 061 2614 224; www.bus-sur.cl) and other companies pick up at the airport after leaving Punta Arenas. In January/February you are advised to book ahead, where possible, as buses do fill up, and there is a possibility that you won't get a seat if starting from the airport. There are **ATMs** at the airport as well as in Punta Arenas itself – you are advised to use these rather than relying on those in Puerto Natales (which frequently run out) for cash required for your trek. Buses pick up and drop off outside their respective offices in Punta Arenas. Fares to Puerto Natales are about $6,000 single or $11,000 return.

Accommodation

There's no shortage of places to stay in Punta Arenas. The following are recommended:

Hostal Art Nouveau
Lautaro Navarro 762
tel 061 2228 112
www.hostalartnouveau.cl

Hostal La Estancia
O'Higgins 765
tel 061 2321 435
www.estancia.cl

Good, friendly place with spacious rooms and dorms in a rambling old house

Hostal Sonia Kuscevic
Pasaje Darwin 175
tel 061 2248 543
www.hostalsk.cl
Long-established *residential*, a short walk from the centre, near the museum and the cemetery

Hotel Plaza
José Nogueira 1116
tel 061 2241 300
www.hotelplaza.cl
Nice small hotel in a historic building the town centre, overlooking the plaza

Where to eat
No shortage of places to eat, either. Highly recommended are **La Luna** (O'Higgins 1017; tel 228 555; www.laluna.cl), an atmospheric and hugely popular place serving a range of dishes (and plenty of wines), including excellent *chupe de centolla*; and **El Mercado** (Mejicana 617, second floor), a well-hidden local favourite serving excellent seafood in as unpretentious surroundings as you'll find.

What to see
While in Punta Arenas it is well worth making a trip to **Isla Magdalena**, a national reserve in the Straits of Magellan and home to some 120,000 Magellanic penguins. **COMAPA** (Lautaro Navarro 1112; tel 061 2200 200; www.comapa.com) runs daily excursions to the island between December and March aboard the *Melinka*, departing from the port north of the cemetery (take a taxi or a *colectivo* – shared taxi – from the town centre) at 3pm. The journey takes about 2hrs each way, and you have 1hr on the island itself. You can get surprisingly close to the birds, but avoid disturbing them. There's no accommodation on the island.

Also not to be missed is the cemetery on **Avenida Manuel Bulnes**, a fascinating testament to town's history. The nearby **Museo Salesiano** (Avenida Manuel Bulnes 336) has interesting displays of artefacts from the local Fuegian Indians.

Transport
Bus companies running services to Puerto Natales include:

Buses Fernández
Armando Sanhueza 745
tel 061 2242 313
www.busesfernandez.com

Buses Pacheco
Avenida Colon 900
tel 061 2242 174
www.busespacheco.com

Bus-Sur
José Menéndez 552
tel 061 2614 224
www.bus-sur.cl

APPENDIX B
Accommodation within Torres del Paine national park

Refugios and campsites

Note: 'Serviced' campsites have showers (usually hot) and toilets; 'unserviced' sites have a toilet only, and sometimes a guardería (ranger's office) and simple shelter.

Name	Type	Meals	Shop	Walk	Contact details
Refugio Paine Grande (Refugio Pehoé)	Hut with about 100 beds, and serviced campsite	Y	Y	1, 2	Vertice, tel 061 2412 742 or 061 2415 693, www.verticepatagonia.com
Campamento Italiano	Unserviced camp-site (free)			1, 2	
Campamento/Domos Francés	Serviced campsite and 3 geodomes (sleeping 8 people each)	Y		1, 2	Fantastico Sur, tel 061 2614 184, www.fantasticosur.com
Refugio Los Cuernos	Beds in hut plus several cabins, and serviced campsite	Y		1, 2	Fantastico Sur, tel 061 2614 184, www.fantasticosur.com
Refugio Las Torres	Two huts (Torre Central, 60 beds, and the older Torre Norte, 62 beds), and serviced campsite	Y	Y	1, 2	Fantastico Sur, tel 061 2614 184, www.fantasticosur.com

Name	Type	Meals	Shop	Walk	Contact details
Refugio El Chileno	Beds in hut, and serviced campsite	Y		1, 2	Fantastico Sur, tel 061 2614 184, www.fantasticosur.com
Campamento Serón	Partly serviced campsite	Y (with advance notice)		1	Fantastico Sur, tel 061 2614 184, www.fantasticosur.com
Refugio Dickson	Hut with 30 beds, serviced campsite	Y		1	Vertice, tel 061 2412 742 or 061 2415 693, www.verticepatagonia.com
Campamento Los Perros	Partly serviced campsite			1	Vertice, tel 061 2412 742 or 061 2415 693, www.verticepatagonia.com
Campamento Paso	Unserviced campsite (free)			1	
Refugio Grey	Hut with 30 beds, serviced campsite	Y		1, 2	Vertice, tel 061 2412 742 or 061 2415 693, www.verticepatagonia.com
Campamento Zapata	Unserviced campsite (free)			7	

Name	Type	Meals	Shop	Walk	Contact details
Camping Pehoé (Area de Acampar Lago Pehoé)	Serviced campsite (can fill up completely in summer, so best to book)	Y	Y	6 (3, 4, 5)	tel 02 196 0377; main office in Punta Arenas tel 061 2249 581, www.campingpehoe.com
Camping Río Serrano	Serviced campsite, about 6km S of CONAF Administración office	Y			www.horseridingpatagonia.com

Ecocamps

	Walk	Contact
Ecocamp Patagonia	Comfortable geodome and an impressive commitment to the environment	1, 2	tel 02 2923 5950 or 0800 051 7095 (toll free from UK), www.ecocamp.travel

Hotels

Name		Walk	Contact
Hotel Las Torres	Large upmarket hotel complex on the Circuit and the 'W'	1, 2	tel 061 2617 450 or 061 2617 451, www.lastorres.com
Hostería Lago Grey	Upmarket hotel at S end of Lago Grey	7	tel 061 2712 100, www.turismolagogrey.com
Hostería Mirador del Paine	Part of old estancia, by Laguna Verde	5	tel 061 2226 930, www.miradordelpayne.com
Posada Río Serrano	Part of old estancia, by Lago Toro	1, 4, 5	Calle Baquedano 534, Puerto Natales, tel 061 2613 531
Hostería Pehoé	Upmarket hotel on island in Lago Pehoé		www.pehoe.cl
Hotel Explora	Upmarket hotel by Lago Pehoé (fully inclusive stays from 4–8 nights)		www.explora.com

APPENDIX C

Language notes and glossary

Chilean Spanish tends to be spoken at truly breakneck pace – and even Castilian Spanish speakers may have difficulty following it.

There are quite a number of words and idioms in Chilean Spanish which differ from standard Castilian Spanish, and the pronunciation can also be something of a hurdle, with consonants being frequently dropped. It also contains a rich vocabulary of slang. Learning a little Castilian Spanish will get you a long way, but you can improve your understanding greatly – and provide a source of great amusement when trying them out – by learning a few of these *chilenismos*. English is widely spoken in *refugios*, hotels and *pensions*; less so by bus and taxi drivers.

As in Castilian Spanish, a number of letters are pronounced quite differently to their familiar sound in English:

c	pronounced soft (like 's') before e or i
h	always silent (not pronounced)
j	pronounced as a guttural 'h', as in *jamón*
ll	pronounced 'y', as in *tortilla*
ñ	pronounced 'ny', as in *mañana*
r	always pronounced rolled
v	pronounced more like 'b'
z	pronounced as a soft 'c', as in **cerveza**

Nouns and adjectives can be masculine, feminine or neuter.

Basic greetings and phrases

English	Spanish
Hello	*Hola*
Good morning	*Buenos días*
Good afternoon	*Buenas tardes*
Good evening, Good night	*Buenas noches*
Goodbye	*Hasta luego or Adiós*

English	Spanish
Bye (informal)	*Ciao*
How are you?	*¿Cómo estás?*
Fine, thank you	*Bien, gracias*
Yes	*Sí*
No	*No*
Please	*Por favor*
Thank you (very much)	*(Muchas) gracias*
You're welcome	*De nada*
Excuse me	*Discúlpeme, perdón*
Sorry	*Lo siento*
Do you speak English?	*¿Habla (usted) inglés?*
I don't speak Spanish	*No hablo español*
I'm English/Irish/Scottish	*Soy inglés(a)/irlandés(a)/escocés(a)*
My name is…	*Me llamo…*
What's your name?	*¿Cómo se llama usted?*
Pleased to meet you	*Mucho gusto*
Do you have…? ('Is there…?' Also in the non-interrogative sense, 'There is…')	*¿Hay…?*
How much does it cost?	*¿Cuánto es?*
I'd like…	*Quisiera…*
I want…	*Quiero…*
Can one…?	*¿Se puede…?*
What?	*¿Qué?*
When?	*¿Cuándo?*
Where is…?	*¿Dónde está…?*
good, bad	*bueno, malo*
with, without	*con, sin*
this, that	*este/a, ese/a*
these, those	*estos/as, esos/as*
here, there	*aquí, allí*
open, closed	*abierto, cerrado*
more, less	*más, menos*
now, later	*ahora, después*

English	Spanish
Numerals	
0	*cero*
1	*un/una/uno*
2	*dos*
3	*tres*
4	*cuatro*
5	*cinco*
6	*seis*
7	*siete*
8	*ocho*
9	*nueve*
10	*diez*
11	*once*
12	*doce*
13	*trece*
14	*catorce*
15	*quince*
16	*dieciséis*
17	*diecisiete*
18	*dieciocho*
19	*diecenueve*
20	*veinte*
21	*veintiuno*
22	*veintidós*
30	*treinta*
40	*cuarenta*
50	*cincuenta*
60	*sesenta*
70	*setenta*
80	*ochenta*
90	*noventa*
100	*cien/ciento*
101	*ciento uno*
200	*doscientos*
500	*quinientos*
1000	*mil*
2000	*dos mil*

English	Spanish
2545	*dos mil quinientos cuaretna cinco*
1 million	*un millión*
Time and dates	
What time is it?	*¿Qué hora es?*
At what time?	*¿A qué hora?*
At…	*A…*
1300	*Es la una*
0800	*Son las ocho*
0815	*Son las ocho y cuarto*
1240	*Es la una menos cuarto*
1500	*Son las tres*
1630	*Son las cuatro y media*
minute	*minuto*
hour	*hora*
day	*día*
week	*semana*
month	*mes*
year	*año*
Monday	*lunes*
Tuesday	*martes*
Wednesday	*miércoles*
Thursday	*jueves*
Friday	*viernes*
Saturday	*sábado*
Sunday	*domingo*
January	*enero*
February	*febrero*
March	*marzo*
April	*abril*
May	*mayo*
June	*junio*
July	*julio*
August	*agosto*
September	*septiembre*
October	*octubre*

English	Spanish
November	*noviembre*
December	*diciembre*
spring	*primavera*
summer	*verano*
autumn	*otoño*
winter	*invierno*
today	*hoy*
tomorrow	*mañana*
yesterday	*ayer*
morning	*mañana*
afternoon	*tarde*
evening	*noche*
night	*noche*

Trekking

English	Spanish
bridge	*puente*
camping	*campamento*
campsite	*zona de acampar*
drinking water	*agua potable*
ford	*vado*
forest	*bosque*
glacier	*glaciar*
high	*alto*
hut	*refugio*
lake	*lago*
mountain	*montaña*
pass	*paso*
path, trail	*sendero*
peak	*cerro, monte*
rain	*lluvia*
ravine	*barranco*
river	*río*
rock	*roca*
steep	*empinado*
stream	*arroyo*
tree	*árbol*
warden/ranger	*guarda*

English	Spanish
warden's/ranger's hut	*guardería*
waterfall	*salto, cascada*
wind	*viente*
Can I camp here?	*¿Se puede acampar aquí?*

Plants and animals

English	Spanish
animal	*animal*
bird	*ave, pájaro*
bushes	*arbusto*
cat	*gato*
condor	*cóndor*
cormorant	*yeco*
dog	*perro*
duck	*pato*
flamingo	*flamenco*
fox	*zorro*
grass	*pasto*
grebe	*huala*
horse	*caballo*
lesser rhea	*nandú*
penguin	*pingüino*
puma	*puma*
rabbit	*conejo*
southern lapwing	*queltehue, tero*
swan	*cisne*
woodpecker	*carpintero*

Travel and accommodation

English	Spanish
ATM	*cajero automático*
bank	*banco*
chemist	*la farmacia*
city, town	*ciudad*
exchange office	*cambia*
grill, steakhouse	*parilla, asado*
hostel	*hostal*
hotel	*hotel*

English	Spanish
laundrette	*lavandería*
market	*mercado*
passport	*pasaporte*
petrol station	*estatción de bencina*
police station	*comisaría*
post office	*correo*
receipt	*recibo*
reservation	*reservación*
restaurant	*restaurante*
room	*habitación*
single room	*habitación para una persona*
double room	*habitación para dos personas*
double bed	*matrimonial*
two beds	*con dos camas*
shared bathroom	*baño compartido*
en suite bathroom	*baño privado*
road	*carretera*
shop	*tienda*
street	*calle*
supermarket	*supermercado*
toilet	*baño*
Do you have a room…?	*¿Tiene una habitación…?*
For one night /two nights/ one week	*Para una noche /dos noches/ una semana*
How much does it cost?	*¿Cuánto es?*
Do you have something cheaper?	*¿Hay algo más barato?*
What time does the bus to… leave?	*¿A qué hora sale el autobús para…?*
What time does it arrive?	*¿A qué hora llega?*

English	Spanish
What time is the bus to…?	*¿A qué hora sale el autobús para…?*
Where does it leave from?	*¿De dónde sale?*

Transport

aeroplane	*avión*
aisle	*pasillo*
airport	*aeropuerto*
bicycle	*bicicleta*
boat (ferry)	*barco (transbordator)*
bus	*autobús*
car	*auto, coche*
petrol	*bencina, gasoline*
platform	*andén*
return ticket	*billete, pasaje de ida y vuelta*
seat	*asiento*
station	*estación, terminal*
ticket	*billete, pasaje*
train	*tren*
window	*ventana*

Equipment

camping gas cartridge	*cartucho de gas*
guidebook	*guía*
hiking boots	*botas de montaña*
jacket	*chaqueta*
map	*mapa*
rucksack, pack	*mochila*
sleeping bag	*saco de dormir*
sleeping mat	*colchoneta*
sun cream	*filtro solar*
tent	*tienda*

English	Spanish
Food and drink	
breakfast	*desayuno*
lunch	*almuerzo*
dinner	*cena*
afternoon tea	*once*
entree	*entrada*
main course	*principal*
desert	*postre*
set menu	*menú del día*
fish	*pescado*
marinated raw fish	*ceviche*
seafood broth	*paila*
white-fleshed fish	
(not conger eel!)	*congrio*
hake	*merluza*
grilled	*a la parilla, al asado*
fried	*a la plancha*
baked	*al horno*
very spicy	*pil-pil*
stew	*estofado*
shellfish	*mariscos*
king crab	*centolla*
king crab cooked in	
white wine, cream and	*chupe de*
breadcrumbs	*centolla*
meat	*carne*
chop or cutlet	*chuleta*
beef	*vacuno*
fillet steak	*filete*
steak	*lomo*
pork	*cerdo*
chicken	*pollo*
rabbit	*conejo*
vegetables	*verdures*
vegetarian	*vegetariano*
salad	*ensalada*

English	Spanish
salad with tomato	
and onion	*ensalada Chilena*
mixed salad	*ensalada surtida*
lettuce	*lechuga*
tomato	*tomate*
onion	*cebolla*
French fries	*papas fritas*
drink	*bebida*
coffee	*café*
tea	*té*
juice	*jugo*
mineral water	*agua*
(still/sparkling)	*(sin gas/con gas)*
fruit	*frutas*
dried fruit	*fruta seca*
nuts	*nuez*
orange	*naranja*
apple	*manzana*
plum	*ciruela*
quince	*membrillo*
wine (red/white)	*vino (tinto/blanco)*
beer	*cerveza*
pisco	*sour*
bread	*pan*
filled pastry	*empañada*
cheese	*queso*
eggs	*huevos*
milk	*leche*
butter	*mantequilla*
jam	*marmelada*
salt	*sal*
pepper	*pimienta*
biscuit	*galleta*
chocolate	*chocolate*
tinned	*enlatado*
soup	*sopa*

English	Spanish
pasta	*pasta*
rice	*arroz*
sugar	*azúcar*
menu	*carta*
Can I have the bill, please?	*La cuenta, por favor*

Emergencies

English	Spanish
accident	*accidente*
broken	*roto*

English	Spanish
danger	*peligro*
doctor	*médico*
fallen	*caido*
Help!	*¡Ayuda!*
hospital	*hospital*
insurance	*seguro*
police	*policía*
unconscious	*inconsciente*

British Embassy
Av El Bosque Norte 0125
Las Condes
Santiago
tel 02 2370 4100
www.britemb.cl

United States Embassy
Av. Andrés Bello 2800
Las Condes
Santiago
tel 02 2330 3000
https://cl.usembassy.gov/

Canadian Embassy
Nueva Tajamar 481 – Piso 12,
Torre Norte
PO Box 139-10
Santiago
tel 02 2652 3800
www.canadainternational.gc.ca/
chile chili

Australian Embassy
Isidora Goyenechea 3621, 13th Floor
Las Condes
Santiago
tel 02 2550 3500
www.chile.embassy.gov.au

French Embassy
Condell 65
Providencia
Santiago
tel 02 2470 8000
www.ambafrance-cl.org

German Embassy
Las Hualtatas 5677
Vitacura
Casilla 220, Correo 30
Santiago
tel 02 2463 2500
www.santiago.diplo.de

Dutch Embassy
Av Apoquindo 3500, Piso 13
Las Condes
Santiago
tel 02 2756 9200
chili.nlambassade.org

CONAF
(Corporación Nacional Forestal,
which manages the national parks)
Av Presidente Bulnes 291
Santiago
www.conaf.cl

Sernatur
(Chilean National Tourist Service)
Av Providencia 1550
Santiago
www.sernatur.cl

DIFROL
(Dirección Nacional de Fronteras
y Límites del Estado, which issues
climbing permits)
Teatinos 180, Piso 7
Santiago
www.difrol.gob.cl

Parque Nacional Torres del Paine
(CONAF's official website for
Torres del Paine national park)
www.parquetorresdelpaine.cl

General information
Torres del Paine:
www.torresdelpaine.com

Chile:
www.chile-travel.com (official
website) and www.gochile.cl

Los Glaciares national park,
El Calafate and El Chaltén:
www.losglaciares.com,
www.calafate.com
and www.elchalten.com

Santiago Times
(the capital's English language
newspaper)
www.santiagotimes.cl

Chile Flora
(excellent website on Chilean flora)
www.chileflora.com

For further information on Chile's
plantlife see: Chilebosque
www.chilebosque.cl

Insectos de Chile
(website dedicated to insects found
in Chile)
www.insectos.cl

Laboratoria de Glaciología
(useful website on Chile's vast glaciers)
www.glaciologia.cl

Gobierno de Chile
(Chilean government website)
www.gob.cl

LATA
(Latin American Travel Association)
www.lata.travel

Turismo Chile
chile.travel

Low cloud over the Paine massif, seen across Lago Pehoé (Walk 1)

Trekking and mountaineering guidebooks

Randonnées Chiliennes by Dominique Argenson (Apostrophes Ediciones, 2003) has a good selection of day walks around Santiago. *Salto Grande – Sendero de Interpretación* (CONAF, no date) is a nice little booklet on Salto Grande, although it's getting fairly hard to find. For those planning a trip to Aconcagua there is Jim Ryan's *Aconcagua and the Southern Andes – A Trekkers Guidebook* (Cicerone, 2nd edition 2009), which also has details of hikes close to Santiago. *The Andes: A Trekking Guide* by John & Cathy Biggar (Andes, 2nd edition 2001) is an excellent guide to over 30 treks throughout the Andes, including several in Patagonia. *Trekking in the Andes* by Val Pitkethly & Kate Harper (New Holland, 2nd edition 2008) is another excellent guide, covering 26 treks and 18 climbing routes in the Andes, including several in Chile and Argentina (New Holland, 2008). Lonely Planet's *Trekking in Patagonia* includes a section on Torres del Paine. John Biggar's *The Andes: A Guide for Climbers* by (Andes, 3rd edition 2005) is a comprehensive guide to climbing throughout the Andes on over 300 peaks including all the 6000ers. For further details on hiking in Argentina's Los Glaciares national park, see Colin Henderson's *Los Glaciares National Park – Travel and Trekking Guide* (Zager & Urruty, 2007), and *Trekking en Chaltén* by Miguel Alonso (Spanish and English, Zagier & Urruty, 1998).

General guidebooks

Of the many general guides available, the *Rough Guide Chile* and *Moon Handbooks Chile* are very reliable and informative.

Travel, exploration and mountaineering

There are numerous works on the early exploration of Patagonia and later mountaineering: Charles Darwin's *Journal of researches into the geology and natural history of the various countries visited by H.M.S. Beagle*, better known through later editions as *Voyage of the Beagle* (Henry Colburn, 1839; Penguin, 1989); Francisco Moreno, *Viaje a la Patagonia Austral* (Buenos Aires, 1879); Lady Florence Dixie, *Across Patagonia* (London, 1880); Julius Beerbohm, *Wanderings in Patagonia* (1879; repr. Nonsuch 2005); W.H. Hudson, *Idle Days in Patagonia* (London, 1893; repr. Nonsuch 2005); George C. Musters, *At Home with the Patagonians* (London, 1871; repr. Nonsuch 2005); Alberto de Agostini, *Andes Patagónicos. Viajes de Exploracion a la Cordillera Patagonica Austral* (Buenos Aires, 1941); Walter Bonatti, *Solitudini Australi* (Club Alpino Italiano, Torino, 1999).

Eric Shipton, *Land of Tempest. Travels in Patagonia 1958–62* (London, 1963) describes the author's epic crossing of the Southern Ice Field, and H.W. Tilman's *Mischief in Patagonia* (Cambridge, 1937) recounts his east–west crossing from his boat, '*Mischief*'. Walter Bonatti's *The Mountains of My Life* (Modern Library, 2001) also has sections dealing with Patagonia, and Simon Yates' *Against the Wall* (Vintage, 1998) recounts an attempt on Torre Central. There's also Alan Kearney, *Mountaineering in Patagonia* (The Mountaineers, 1993).

Best-known of all travel books on Patagonia is Bruce Chatwin's hugely influential *In Patagonia* (London, 1977) – which you can place nicely into context by visiting Cueva del Milodón near Torres del Paine, and passing by the house in Punta Arenas where his great-uncle, Charley Milward, once lived; more recently there is Sara Wheeler, *Travels in a Thin Country* (London, 1994).

Perhaps the finest book on Patagonia, however, is Lucas Bridges' *Uttermost Part of the Earth* (London,

Small waterfall in the Valle Ascencio, Torresdel Paine national park (Walks 1 and 2)

1948; repr. Century, 1987), a heartfelt and deeply moving account of the author's early life and exploration in Tierra del Fuego, his contact with the local Fuegian tribes, and their gradual, inevitable submergence beneath the approaching tide of 'civilization'. If you only take one book with you on your travels to Patagonia, make it this one.

History and ethnography

S. Collier & W. Sater, *A History of Chile, 1801–1994* (Cambridge, 2004); S. Villalobos, *A Short History of Chile* (Santiago, 1996); Mateo Martinic, *Brief History of the Land of Magellan* (Punta Arenas, 2002); Chris Moss, *Patagonia. A Cultural History* (Landscapes of the Imagination series, Signal Books, Oxford 2008); Colin McEwan, Luis Alberto Borrero & Alfredo Prieto, *History, Prehistory and Ethnography at the Uttermost End of the Earth* (London, BM Press, 1997); Nick Reding, *The Last Cowboys at the End of the World – The Story of the Gauchos of Patagonia* (Crown, 2001).

Folklore, myths and legends

Mario Echeverría Baleta, *Tehuelche Life and Legends* (trans. C.A. Fox, Punta Arenas, 2003); J. Wilbert & K. Simoneau, *Folk Literature of the Tehuelche Indians* (Los Angeles, 1984).

Literature and poetry

Pablo Neruda, *Selected Poems – A Bilingual Edition* (Jonathan Cape, 1970; Penguin, 1975) is a good introduction to the work of Chile's Nobel Prize winning poet. A good collection of Gabriela Mistral's poetry is *Selected Poems* (University of New Mexico Press, 2003); Mistral was the first Latin American writer to be awarded the Nobel Prize for Literature. Many of Ariel Dorfman's works have been translated into English, including his most famous play, *Death and the Maiden*, and the autobiographical *Heading South, Looking North*. Isabelle Allende's novels translated into English include *The House of the Spirits* and *Eva Luna*.

Language

Dictionaries and phrasebooks include *Chilenismos: A Dictionary and Phrasebook for Chilean Spanish* (Hippocrene NY, 2005), by Daniel Joelson, and the Rough Guide's *Latin American Phrasebook* (Rough Guide, 2006). Language courses include *Teach Yourself Latin American Spanish* (Teach Yourself Books, 2003). Oxford and Collins both publish good pocket-sized English–Spanish dictionaries.

One of the most famous books on the language of the Fuegian Indians is *Yamana–English Dictionary*, a unique and fascinating lexicon written over many years by the Rev. Thomas Bridges, father of Lucas Bridges (who went on to write *Uttermost Part of the Earth*). The only manuscript of the book was stolen by the polar explorer Frederick Cook, lost during two world wars in Europe, and finally discovered in a farmhouse kitchen cupboard, and now resides in the British Library.

Photographs
Among the many photographic works on the wild landscapes of southern Chile and Patagonia are Hubert Stadler & Michael Allhof, *Patagonia* (C.J. Bucher Verlag, 2006); Marcos Zimmermann, *Patagonia: Nature's Last Frontier* (New Holland, 2007); and Daniel Rivademar & Alejandro Winograd, *Patagonia: Land of Giants* (Island Press, 2004).

Wildlife and plants
An excellent (albeit somewhat expensive given its size) all-round guide to wildlife, birds and plants of the national park is Gladys Garay & Oscar Guineo, *Fauna, Flora y Montaña Torres del Paine* (English/Spanish, Punta Arenas, 2006). This is an expanded and updated form of the same authors' earlier work (covering animals and birds only), *Conociendo la Fauna de Torres del Paine/The Fauna of Torres del Paine* (Punta Arenas, 1997).

Sharon Chester, *A Wildlife Guide to Chile: Continental Chile, Chilean Antarctica, Easter Island, Juan Fernandez Archipelago* (Princeton University Press, Princeton, New Jersey, 2008) is an outstanding general guide to the natural history of Chile – from birds and mammals to butterflies, fish and plant life.

Bird-watchers are well catered for, since there are some truly excellent field guides available. Top of the list are Alvaro Jaramillo, Peter Burke & David Beadle, *Birds of Chile: Including the Antarctic Peninsular, the Falkland Islands and South Georgia* (Helm Field Guides, 2003; Princeton University Press, 2003); and Martín R de la Peña & Maurice Rumboll, *Birds of Southern South America and Antarctica* (Princeton University Press, Princeton, New Jersey, 2008; originally published as *Collins Illustrated Checklist: Birds of Southern South America and Antarctica*, Collins, 1998).

Another handy guide, also easily obtainable in Chile, is Enrique Couve & Claudio F. Vidal, *Birds/Aves Torres del Paine. Guía de Campo/Field Guide* (English/Spanish; second edition, Editorial Fantástico Sur, Punta Arenas, 2004, repr. 2007) – although it doesn't match the Princeton and Helm guides mentioned above.

Now out of print, Graham Harris, *A Guide to the Birds and Mammals of Coastal Patagonia* (Princeton, 1998) is another more general guide to the area.

Lapidatrists are directed to Luis E. Peña G. and Alfredo J. Ugarte P., *Las Mariposas de Chile/The Butterflies of Chile* (out of print; Editorial Universitaria, Santiago, 1996), if they can find a copy; or the relevant section of Sharon Chester's book. Butterflies and other insects are listed on www.insectos.cl (Spanish language only).

For plants in Torres del Paine, the most easily obtainable field guide is Osvaldo Vidal O., *Flora Torres del Paine. Guía de Campo/Field Guide* (English/Spanish; Editorial Fantástico Sur, Punta Arenas, 2007). CONAF produces a series of small guides to Chilean trees and other plants (and animals), in theory available from their office in Santiago but in practice frustratingly difficult to obtain.

There are also some very useful websites dedicated to the plantlife of Chile. These include Chilebosque, www.chilebosque.cl (Spanish, some parts in English). Most useful of all, however, is Chileflora, www.chileflora.com (English, with an excellent search page).

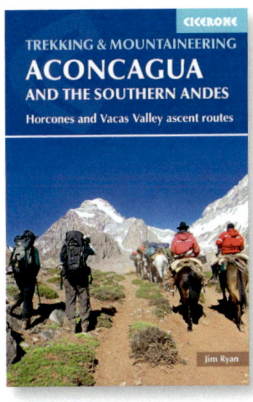

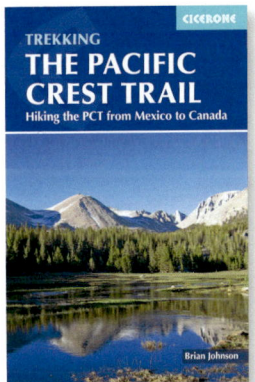

LISTING OF CICERONE GUIDES

SCOTLAND

Backpacker's Britain:
    Northern Scotland
Ben Nevis and Glen Coe
Cycling in the Hebrides
Great Mountain Days in Scotland
Mountain Biking in Southern
    and Central Scotland
Mountain Biking in West and
    North West Scotland
Not the West Highland Way
Scotland
Scotland's Best Small Mountains
Scotland's Far West
Scotland's Mountain Ridges
Scrambles in Lochaber
The Ayrshire and Arran
    Coastal Paths
The Border Country
The Cape Wrath Trail
The Great Glen Way
The Great Glen Way Map Booklet
The Hebridean Way
The Hebrides
The Isle of Mull
The Isle of Skye
The Skye Trail
The Southern Upland Way
The Speyside Way
The Speyside Way Map Booklet
The West Highland Way
Walking Highland Perthshire
Walking in Scotland's Far North
Walking in the Angus Glens
Walking in the Cairngorms
Walking in the Ochils, Campsie
    Fells and Lomond Hills
Walking in the Pentland Hills
Walking in the Southern Uplands
Walking in Torridon
Walking Loch Lomond
    and the Trossachs
Walking on Arran
Walking on Harris and Lewis
Walking on Jura, Islay and Colonsay
Walking on Rum and the Small Isles
Walking on the Orkney
    and Shetland Isles
Walking on Uist and Barra
Walking the Corbetts
    Vol 1 South of the Great Glen
Walking the Corbetts
    Vol 2 North of the Great Glen
Walking the Galloway Hills
Walking the Munros
    Vol 1 – Southern, Central
    and Western Highlands

Walking the Munros
    Vol 2 – Northern Highlands
    and the Cairngorms
West Highland Way Map Booklet
Winter Climbs Ben Nevis
    and Glen Coe
Winter Climbs in the Cairngorms

NORTHERN ENGLAND TRAILS

Hadrian's Wall Path
Hadrian's Wall Path Map Booklet
Pennine Way Map Booklet
The Coast to Coast Map Booklet
The Coast to Coast Walk
The Dales Way
The Dales Way Map Booklet
The Pennine Way

LAKE DISTRICT

Cycling in the Lake District
Great Mountain Days in
    the Lake District
Lake District Winter Climbs
Lake District: High Level
    and Fell Walks
Lake District: Low Level
    and Lake Walks
Lakeland Fellranger
Mountain Biking in the Lake District
Scrambles in the Lake District
    – North and South
Short Walks in Lakeland
    Book 1: South Lakeland
Short Walks in Lakeland
    Book 2: North Lakeland
Short Walks in Lakeland
    Book 3: West Lakeland
Tour of the Lake District
Trail and Fell Running in
    the Lake District

NORTH WEST ENGLAND
AND THE ISLE OF MAN

Cycling the Pennine Bridleway
Cycling the Way of the Roses
Isle of Man Coastal Path
The Lancashire Cycleway
The Lune Valley and Howgills
The Ribble Way
Walking in Cumbria's Eden Valley
Walking in Lancashire
Walking in the Forest of
    Bowland and Pendle
Walking on the Isle of Man
Walking on the West
    Pennine Moors
Walks in Lancashire Witch Country

Walks in Ribble Country
Walks in Silverdale and Arnside

NORTH EAST ENGLAND,
YORKSHIRE DALES
AND PENNINES

Cycling in the Yorkshire Dales
Great Mountain Days
    in the Pennines
Mountain Biking in the
    Yorkshire Dales
South Pennine Walks
St Oswald's Way and St
    Cuthbert's Way
The Cleveland Way and the
    Yorkshire Wolds Way
The Cleveland Way Map Booklet
The North York Moors
The Reivers Way
The Teesdale Way
Walking in County Durham
Walking in Northumberland
Walking in the North Pennines
Walking in the Yorkshire
    Dales: North and East
Walking in the Yorkshire
    Dales: South and West
Walks in Dales Country
Walks in the Yorkshire Dales

WALES AND WELSH BORDERS

Glyndwr's Way
Great Mountain Days in Snowdonia
Hillwalking in Shropshire
Hillwalking in Wales – Vol 1
Hillwalking in Wales – Vol 2
Mountain Walking in Snowdonia
Offa's Dyke Path
Offa's Dyke Map Booklet
Pembrokeshire Coast
    Path Map Booklet
Ridges of Snowdonia
Scrambles in Snowdonia
The Ascent of Snowdon
The Ceredigion and
    Snowdonia Coast Paths
The Pembrokeshire Coast Path
The Severn Way
The Snowdonia Way
The Wales Coast Path
The Wye Valley Walk
Walking in Carmarthenshire
Walking in Pembrokeshire
Walking in the Forest of Dean
Walking in the South Wales Valleys
Walking in the Wye Valley
Walking on the Brecon Beacons

Walking on the Gower
Welsh Winter Climbs

DERBYSHIRE, PEAK DISTRICT AND MIDLANDS

Cycling in the Peak District
Dark Peak Walks
Scrambles in the Dark Peak
Walking in Derbyshire
White Peak Walks: The Northern Dales
White Peak Walks: The Southern Dales

SOUTHERN ENGLAND

20 Classic Sportive Rides in South East England
20 Classic Sportive Rides in South West England
Cycling in the Cotswolds
Mountain Biking on the North Downs
Mountain Biking on the South Downs
North Downs Way Map Booklet
South West Coast Path Map Booklet – Minehead to St Ives
South West Coast Path Map Booklet – Plymouth to Poole
South West Coast Path Map Booklet – St Ives to Plymouth
Suffolk Coast and Heath Walks
The Cotswold Way
The Cotswold Way Map Booklet
The Great Stones Way
The Kennet and Avon Canal
The Lea Valley Walk
The North Downs Way
The Peddars Way and Norfolk Coast Path
The Pilgrims' Way
The Ridgeway Map Booklet
The Ridgeway National Trail
The South Downs Way
The South Downs Way Map Booklet
The South West Coast Path
The Thames Path
The Thames Path Map Booklet
The Two Moors Way
Walking Hampshire's Test Way
Walking in Cornwall
Walking in Essex
Walking in Kent
Walking in London
Walking in Norfolk
Walking in Sussex
Walking in the Chilterns
Walking in the Cotswolds
Walking in the Isles of Scilly

Walking in the New Forest
Walking in the North Wessex Downs
Walking in the Thames Valley
Walking on Dartmoor
Walking on Guernsey
Walking on Jersey
Walking on the Isle of Wight
Walking the Jurassic Coast
Walks in the South Downs National Park

BRITISH ISLES CHALLENGES, COLLECTIONS AND ACTIVITIES

The Book of the Bivvy
The Book of the Bothy
The C2C Cycle Route
The End to End Cycle Route
The Mountains of England and Wales: Vol 1 Wales
The Mountains of England and Wales: Vol 2 England
The National Trails
The UK's County Tops
Three Peaks, Ten Tors

ALPS CROSS-BORDER ROUTES

100 Hut Walks in the Alps
Across the Eastern Alps: E5
Alpine Ski Mountaineering Vol 1 – Western Alps
Alpine Ski Mountaineering Vol 2 – Central and Eastern Alps
Chamonix to Zermatt
The Karnischer Höhenweg
The Tour of the Bernina
Tour of Mont Blanc
Tour of Monte Rosa
Tour of the Matterhorn
Trail Running – Chamonix and the Mont Blanc region
Trekking in the Alps
Trekking in the Silvretta and Rätikon Alps
Trekking Munich to Venice
Walking in the Alps

PYRENEES AND FRANCE/SPAIN CROSS-BORDER ROUTES

The GR10 Trail
The GR11 Trail
The Pyrenean Haute Route
The Pyrenees
The Way of St James – Spain
Walks and Climbs in the Pyrenees

AUSTRIA

The Adlerweg
Trekking in Austria's Hohe Tauern
Trekking in the Stubai Alps

Trekking in the Zillertal Alps
Walking in Austria

SWITZERLAND

Cycle Touring in Switzerland
The Swiss Alpine Pass Route – Via Alpina Route 1
The Swiss Alps
Tour of the Jungfrau Region
Walking in the Bernese Oberland
Walking in the Valais
Walks in the Engadine – Switzerland

FRANCE AND BELGIUM

Chamonix Mountain Adventures
Cycle Touring in France
Cycling London to Paris
Cycling the Canal du Midi
Écrins National Park
Mont Blanc Walks
Mountain Adventures in the Maurienne
The GR20 Corsica
The GR5 Trail
The GR5 Trail – Vosges and Jura
The Grand Traverse of the Massif Central
The Loire Cycle Route
The Moselle Cycle Route
The River Rhone Cycle Route
The Robert Louis Stevenson Trail
The Way of St James
Tour of the Oisans: The GR54
Tour of the Queyras
Tour of the Vanoise
Vanoise Ski Touring
Via Ferratas of the French Alps
Walking in Corsica
Walking in Provence – East
Walking in Provence – West
Walking in the Auvergne
Walking in the Briançonnais
Walking in the Cevennes
Walking in the Dordogne
Walking in the Haute Savoie: North
Walking in the Haute Savoie: South
Walks in the Cathar Region
Walking in the Ardennes

GERMANY

Hiking and Biking in the Black Forest
The Danube Cycleway Volume 1
The Rhine Cycle Route
The Westweg
Walking in the Bavarian Alps

For full information on all our
guides, books and eBooks,
visit our website:
www.cicerone.co.uk

Walking – Trekking – Mountaineering – Climbing – Cycling

Over 40 years, Cicerone have built up an outstanding collection of over 300 guides, inspiring all sorts of amazing adventures.

 Every guide comes from extensive exploration and research by our expert authors, all with a passion for their subjects. They are frequently praised, endorsed and used by clubs, instructors and outdoor organisations.

All our titles can now be bought as **e-books**, **ePubs** and **Kindle** files and we also have an online magazine – **Cicerone Extra** – with features to help cyclists, climbers, walkers and trekkers choose their next adventure, at home or abroad.

Our website shows any **new information** we've had in since a book was published. Please do let us know if you find anything has changed, so that we can publish the latest details. On our **website** you'll also find great ideas and lots of detailed information about what's inside every guide and you can buy **individual routes** from many of them online.

It's easy to keep in touch with what's going on at Cicerone by getting our monthly **free e-newsletter**, which is full of offers, competitions, up-to-date information and topical articles. You can subscribe on our home page and also follow us on **Facebook** and **Twitter** or dip into our **blog**.

Cicerone – the very best guides for exploring the world.

CICERONE

Juniper House, Murley Moss, Oxenholme Road, Kendal, Cumbria LA9 7RL
Tel: 015395 62069 info@cicerone.co.uk
www.cicerone.co.uk